NO MERE CHANCE

NO MERE CHANCE

Dr. John Laird

HODDER AND STOUGHTON

and

SCRIPTURE UNION

British Library Cataloguing in Publication Data

Laird, Dr. J.
  No Mere Chance

  1. Evangelists – Biography
  I. Title
  269'.2'0924   BV3785.L/

  ISBN 0 340 26966 9

Hodder and Stoughton Editorial Office: 47 Bedford Square, London WC1B 3DP.

PREFACE

Henry Ford is reported to have declared that history is bunk, but wiser men have disagreed. Churchill's sense of history enabled him to take a wider view and to assess the future more successfully than most of his contemporaries.

The prophet Joel speaks of the old men dreaming their dreams of the past and the young men seeing their visions of the future. They both need each other.

In Roman mythology Janus was the god of doorways. He was portrayed in the form of two heads fused into one, the heads facing opposite directions.

Thus wise men in all ages have learned to combine insight into the past with foresight. Only thus can they be like the men of Issachar who had understanding of the times to know what Israel ought to do (1 Chr. 12:32).

This autobiography is only a minute scrap of contemporary history, but I pray that some of the lessons learned and experiences described may be of use to those who read.

I owe a very deep debt of gratitude to many friends who have been my advisers and friendly critics, but above all to my wife who encouraged me from the beginning and who, when I was tempted to give up in despair, urged me to go on, and worked with me until the job was done.

CONTENTS

1 BEGINNINGS

In the midwinter of 1915, when Europe was in the grip of World War One, our mother died. She was only thirty-four and our father was left with four motherless children of whom I was the eldest, aged ten. I remember little about my mother except her gentleness and sweetness but I still have a manuscript of her poems, nearly all of a deeply Christian nature and perhaps, by our modern standards, very sentimental. She suffered, I believe, from a 'rheumatic heart', a common complaint in Scotland in the old days, and she caught a chill one cold evening while saying farewell to guests at the garden gate. Dr. Peter Laird, our family doctor, but not of our immediate family, called in a Glasgow professor and after he had gone (I was in bed), I heard my father rush upstairs, lock himself in the bathroom and sob his heart out. Next day I gave my mother a whistle for her to blow if she wanted anything. It was tied to her bed with string but to my disappointment she never used it.

Early one morning my father came into the bedroom where my sister Mona and I were in the big double bed. He went over to the mirror with his back to us so that we could not see his tear-stained face, and brushed his hair. I asked, 'How is Mother, Daddy?' In a broken voice he said, 'She's gone.' We hid our heads under the blankets and cried.

Auntie Mary, my mother's sister, dear inarticulate Auntie Mary, patted us gently and all she could think to say in the way of comfort was, 'Never mind, never mind'. At her funeral the village shopkeepers closed their shops briefly and stood sympathetically in their doorways as the mourners passed.

Soon afterwards another sister of my mother's, Auntie Nettie Thomson, came to care for us, and in the years that followed she looked after us well. She was undemonstrative, self-disciplined, perhaps a bit old-fashioned and unimaginative, but loving, devoted and kind.

The blow of our mother's death was much softened because we were part of an extended family, most of whom lived near us, and they included a great-grandmother, two great-aunts, two grandparents, eighteen uncles and aunts and eight cousins. They were all on quite good terms with each other and ready to help in any emergency.

My grandmother wrote me a personal letter of sympathy, in her clear handwriting, on notepaper edged in black. In it she quoted Psalm 27:10, 'When my father and my mother forsake me, then the Lord will take me up'. I was deeply touched by her kindness and secretly rather proud because she had written to me, a ten-year-old, as if I was a responsible grown-up. I kept her letter for many years.

The Laird family had lived in Kilmacolm since at least 1650. So far as we know, they were probably God-fearing country folk who left us an inheritance of faith and good works. My father used to quote the old French motto 'Noblesse oblige'— noble birth imposes the obligations of noble works and actions.

It was in a small stone house, on the hill above the church, that I was born in the early hours of the morning of November 26th, 1905.

My father was an architect and he designed many of the houses in our village. He loved bright colours, so his houses have red roofs, in contrast to the usual sombre slate-grey. His carpenters' shop, with its friendly men working with their power-driven saws and piles of sawdust and shavings, was a constant source of interest to us children, my three sisters and myself

As the family grew, we moved to a larger house. The front windows looked across the wide valley of the Gryffe to Misty Law and Laird's Seat. The Crankle Burn flowed close by, and I built a small dam and watched the minnows and sticklebacks and the funny little caddis grubs crawling on the bottom. One day we found a lark's nest in a field, and on another occasion I chased and caught a baby rabbit. As I held the frightened little animal in my arms before releasing it, a warm trickle descended down the front of my shirt.

The inhabitants of the village in which I was born over seventy years ago were mostly honest, religious folk. In addition to the Auld Kirk there were St. Columba's and St. James's, both Presbyterian churches, St. Fillans, Episcopalian, the Gospel Hall and a small group of Russellites or Millenial Dawn, now known as Jehovah's Witnesses. Grannie Laird was a member of this group. Whatever may have been her beliefs, she brought up her family to fear God and to do what was right, and in all her ways she exemplified all that a fine Christian should be. Our parents belonged to the Gospel Hall while Grandfather Laird and some of his family were members of St. James's, the United Presbyterian Church. In spite of our religious differences we were a united and happy family. From our village life, we looked out on an ordered world, where God was in heaven, the king was on his throne, and the church bells rang out every Sunday. Father was head of the family, and we respected and looked up to the local ministers of the church.

Grandfather John Laird, who was born in 1850, went into business in Glasgow as a stationer and founded the company bearing his name. They made brown paper bags, and I dimly remember long tables with women sitting alongside one another complete with paste pots and brown paper, making each bag by hand.

Grandmother Thomson came from Glasgow after the death of her husband, for Kilmacolm was renowned for its invigorating climate. When she arrived with her seven children there was a lively little mission hall in the village and John Thomson and maybe some other members of the family, almost certainly including Agnes, became happily involved. My warm-hearted father was also part of the mission hall group at the time. He loved the warmth and the fellowship, and Agnes. But the Kilmacolm air didn't benefit Grandmother Thomson and she died of tuberculosis, thus leaving my sisters and myself with no actual contact with our maternal grandparents.

We grew up in the Gospel Hall. From a simple evangelistic mission it became an Open Brethren assembly. We met in an upstairs room overlooking the market place, on the other side of the burn from the kirk. Membership was quite small, maybe twenty to thirty village folk who were respected in their daily work but cut off from the other churches in the village.

In the Gospel Hall on winter mornings, there was a well-stacked, brightly glowing coal fire, and there were occasions

11

when we literally sat around the fire in a half-circle with the table bearing the bread and wine in the centre.

In those days travelling on Sunday was avoided except for emergencies, so our preachers would arrive on Saturday night and leave on Monday morning. Nearly always there were guests in our hospitable home, the only one large enough to entertain visitors on a regular basis. Many, perhaps most, were saintly men who made a deep impression on us as children and later as teenagers. I look back on our family Sundays as peaceful and quietly happy days. Father would conduct family worship after breakfast (we always had kedgeree instead of porridge), and we loved to hear him read the great Bible stories, especially the more melodramatic ones, from the Old Testament.

There was nothing harsh or severely legalistic about our Sundays at home. When we were younger and got a bit too boisterous, Auntie Mary might say, but always with a twinkle in her eye:

> This is Sunday, Sabbath day
> That is why we should not play,
> Run about and make a noise,
> Like the naughty girls and boys.

On one occasion during these formative years I learned a valuable lesson. My father brought home a new bread-cutter. The loaf was put on a wooden base and the slices cut to a regular and even thickness by the cutting edge of a lever. We children were strictly warned not to touch it. Next morning I was up early and into the pantry slicing the bread on the new cutter.

We gathered for breakfast round the kitchen table, Father, Mother, Mona, Martha and, in her high-chair, my youngest sister, Nancy. After Father had said grace he asked, 'Who cut the bread this morning? You were told not to touch the bread-cutter. Did you, Clelland?' (my middle name abbreviated from Maclelland).

'No, Dad,'

Each member of the family except Nancy was asked and all denied. Again I was asked and again said no. But this time

Father pressed the question and I admitted my awful crime. I was taken upstairs to the bathroom and given a good spanking. That was, no doubt, all as it should be, but it was not quite the end of the story. On returning to the kitchen I found my mother in tears and then I really was smitten in my conscience for I realised that she was deeply grieved because I had told a lie. Somehow, ever since then, I have hated falsehood and tried to speak the truth. But I must admit that tactfulness and consideration for the sensibilities of others (sometimes called diplomacy) have since presented dilemmas which have not always been as wisely or as honestly handled as they should have been.

When I was seven, I knelt one evening by my bedside to offer a simple prayer. I wanted to make quite sure that I had committed my life to Christ and that I was accepted by Him. My prayer was quite brief, 'Lord, if I have never before put my trust in Thee as my saviour, I do it now'. The door of my little room was open and my father came in to say good-night and I told him of my prayer. It was the first of many significant decisions and choices that were to follow in later years.

As children we did not find it a hardship to learn passages of Scripture and the Shorter Catechism off by heart. At the time much of it may have been little understood; but it made a splendid foundation and a general framework in which faith would flourish in later years, and in due course we passed this on to our children.

Kilmacolm, with all its traditions and family history remained our home until our mother died. The early days after her death were hard, for war had broken out, and at about the same time my father lost his practice as an architect as private building petered out. Subsequently he got a job with John Laing at Gretna Green, and so we moved south to a terraced house in Dumfries. I was sent to Dumfries Academy, and a year later we moved south again, this time to Whinnyrigg near Annan on the estuary of the Solway. We set up house in a fisherman's cottage with a large vegetable garden. The owners of the cottage, the Bryson family, who were of Brethren persuasion and deeply religious, lived next door, and I remember being given a copy of Proverbs, price a halfpenny, which I used to carry in my jacket pocket and occasionally read at odd moments, sometimes in the lunch hour at school. There is an old saying that the Scots were brought up on porridge and proverbs. This was certainly true of the Brysons, whose breakfast was porridge and quite often their evening meal consisted of salmon, potatoes and milk, mixed together in a large bowl, followed by a reading from the chapter of Proverbs corresponding to the day of the month. There being thirty-one chapters, this proved to be quite a convenient arrangement.

All my life I have valued and treasured wise sayings, proverbs and scraps of poetry, and the one my grandmother gave me on my first day at a new school must have been among the first. She was a stately old lady dressed in black, and sitting by the window of our home she called me over to her. As I stood by her knee, aged ten, she said, 'Now, Clelland, remember: keep calm, cool and collected.'

The Brysons fished for salmon in the Solway Firth. We sometimes walked across a broad stretch of sand to where iron stakes were driven deeply across one of the channels with a poke net between each pair, and the fish swimming out to sea with the rapidly ebbing tide were then caught by the gills. On one occasion a net was nearly carried away and I struggled with old Mr. Bryson and one of his sons to retrieve it. Trudging home across the wet sand I asked the gnarled old man if he thought that my efforts had made any difference in saving the net, to which he replied with his customary caution, 'Well, a few pounds might just have made the difference'. 'A few pounds!' I thought indignantly. But I said nothing.

Whinnyrigg had much to commend it in time of war. We always had plenty to eat and life was peaceful and undisturbed, if somewhat primitive. We clattered noisily to Annan Academy, less than two miles away, wearing our sturdy clogs, and I often dawdled happily homewards through the lush meadows looking for interesting insects, water creatures or flowers.

As a boy in Kilmacolm I used to wear a kilt on special occasions. In these days by the Solway we were very hard up, and my father and aunt felt that the kilt was too good to be abandoned and that I should wear it. In all probability not one boy at Annan Academy had ever been seen in a kilt and when

I appeared in this attire I was greeted with derision. A rather ribald rhyme adapted from a children's skipping song was chanted after me whenever I appeared:

Kiltie, kiltie cauld bum,
Three kicks at his bum,
Yin for you and yin for me
And yin for kiltie cauld bum.

How I hated that kilt. Putting it on one morning in my bedroom I was reduced to tears at the thought of this teasing, and prayed for deliverance that I might be spared the humiliation. But my father was pretty short-tempered with me, for he was under severe strain in those days, poor man, and failed to see the importance of his son's school status. I went into the kitchen to help my aunt with the breakfast when she gently interceded with my irate father on the grounds that after all, I was giving her a helping hand. Somehow I never remember having to wear the kilt again.

Annan Academy in those war days was a rough school. The headmaster was a powerfully built man who could give six of the best with the tawse. I have a vivid memory of his towering over us in the assembly hall which had a strong smell of antiseptic. I was in a class reigned over by a master whom we nicknamed Daddy Mutch. His jackets were too big for him and were frayed around the cuffs. His first duty every morning was to conduct compulsory religious exercises and this consisted of rattling through the fortieth Psalm and the Lord's Prayer at top speed at nine o'clock every day for most of the school year. If our speed showed signs of slacking he chimed in and speeded us on to greater efforts, and thus ended our daily morning 'worship'.

We only stayed at Whinnyrigg for some months before moving to Powfoot also on the Solway, a few miles from Annan. While there I had a pet hedgehog and started keeping nature diaries of a sort. One evening I was planted firmly in the kitchen with a good fire burning and encouraged to get on with some nature project that I was busy with at the time. I had a feeling that my father and my aunt had something very important to discuss in the front room.

15

A few days later the family were given several special announcements. One was that the war was over and to my innocent question, 'Who won?', the adults only laughed, much to my mortification. Then my father announced that he and Aunt Nettie were to be married and how wonderful this would be. But for us the most wonderful part was to hear that we would be returning to Kilmacolm to live in my grand-mother's old home, Summerlea, which had a summer house and a well in the garden.

My father and Auntie Nettie were married in a Glasgow hotel in the summer of 1919, which was quite a usual practice in those days when many weddings took place in the home or in a hotel, with a minister or elder officiating.

And so the war was over and what a war it had been! For sixty million combatants it had been death, muddle, madness, misery and mud; but for us four children it had just meant moving from one place to another until we returned to our old traditional pattern of life.

I travelled daily by train to Glasgow High School and immediately fell under the spell of the novels of Sir Walter Scott which I read on the journey. My three sisters had a good education at St. Columba's Girls' School and Father's architect-ural practice picked up again. The teaching at Glasgow High School at the time was old-fashioned and mediocre, probably because of a shortage of teachers following the war. Travelling home from school one day in the company of another lad, Willie, we took it upon ourselves to slash the luggage rack and upholstery. I didn't really know Willie well enough to know why he felt compelled to instigate this sort of vandalism but the fact is that he did, and I was not strong-minded enough to resist his lead. We were picked up by the police and suffered nothing worse than a very serious warning that if we did it again trouble would ensue. We didn't. This was followed by a somewhat painful interview with my father and that was the end of that. But to this day I sometimes have a rueful twinge of conscience when I see the vandalism on our trains.

One afternoon, on returning from school to Summerlea, I was surprised to find that my stepmother was not around. Going upstairs I noticed that her bedroom door was closed and I heard the sound of her voice. On listening a little more closely I realised that she was praying aloud. This incident had a considerable effect on me. For the first time I came to understand that my stepmother really believed in the power of prayer and practised it, not only in family and church worship but also in private.

Then something happened of far reaching significance.

It was decided that my cousin Ian Laird and I were to go to school in England. Father had a friend who had sons at Bootham, the Quaker school at York, and he told my father that if he had six sons he would send them all there. His enthusiasm obviously influenced my father and Uncle Nigel so much that my cousin and I went to Bootham in September 1920.

Our headmaster was Arthur Rowntree a member of the well-known Quaker family. By September 1920, the war being over, he had gathered round him an outstanding team, each one a character in his own right, and for the first time I had teachers who inspired me. Leslie Gilbert was my favourite. His teaching of history, especially the period of the Industrial Revolution, aroused indignation, pity and a challenge to do something. I put all I knew into the history essays I wrote for him and got full marks nearly every time.

Arthur Rowntree used to say that, 'The test of a true education is what a man does when he is not compelled to do anything.' We learned that the use of leisure was important and every boy was encouraged to have a hobby. Prizes were given, not for school lessons but for good work in creative activities.

My father came to visit me at Bootham and I took him to see York Minster. As an architect and a lover of beautiful things, his brown eyes sparkled: he was entranced by the beauty of the great east and west windows and the Five Sisters window; the magnificence of the nave and the grandeur of the choir screen. Teasingly, I said, 'Aren't you glad, Dad, that it wasn't Gospel Halls all down through the ages?' He laughed, and called me a naughty boy.

The year 1922 is an important landmark in my memory for it was in that summer holiday that I went to my first Scripture Union camp. My stepmother and her family had long associations with the Children's Special Service Mission (CSSM) and Scripture Union, ever since Grandmother Thomson took

17

her children to the earliest CSSM meetings conducted by the founder, Josiah Spiers.

The camp was located near Lochearnhead in Perthshire. The leader, Frank Millard, found a suitable site on some level ground in the bend of a stream near the head of the loch and got permission to use it. In the train on his way home to Glasgow, he realised that he had omitted to measure the site. He feared that the area of level ground might be too restricted and this worried him for several days until he was greatly reassured to read in his *Daily Light* for March 6th, 1922: 'The Lord your God . . . went in the way before you to search you out a place to pitch your tents in . . . The steps of a good man are ordered by the Lord and He delighteth in His way.' In the event the site proved to be ideal.

At the close of each day's games, excursions and outdoor activities, we gathered in the marquee for a meeting led by W. G. Ovens. There were the inevitable choruses, some better than others, and then some clear and relevant teaching on some aspect of Biblical doctrine. On the last night we had testimonies and an appeal when we were asked to stand if we were willing to commit our lives for the first time to Christ as Saviour, or to do so as an act of witness and renewed commitment to Christ as Lord and Master.

This was quite a new approach to me. To take a public stand for the first time in this way was far from easy and I was in a state of inner turmoil, increasingly so as the meeting progressed. One of our campers, a lanky fellow, Knipe by name, was a crack cross-country runner and this held my admiration for I did some running myself. When Knipe stood up, that tipped the scales for me and I followed suit feeling very embarrassed and awkward.

Some of this may be open to criticism but for me, at any rate, it was a major milestone. It was a sincere act of commitment to Jesus Christ and I have never knowingly gone back on it. If, at times, I have been tempted to waver, that schoolboy commitment stands out as a shining moment which I feel I must never betray or go back on. But though it was a definite and public act of commitment that I made, it was for me personally, the climax of the background of teaching and example of earlier days.

About the age of twelve, my stepmother had enrolled me as a member of her Scattered Members' Branch of the Scripture Union. The membership card was printed on green paper with the initial letters *S* and *U* in gold. The daily reading, on a systematic basis of a short passage from the Bible, became a life-long habit and a discipline of inestimable value.

For some sixty years, the daily message covering in an orderly way both Old and New Testaments, and supplemented for most of that period by the expository notes, has descended like a refreshing rain upon my spirit. Day by day there has come challenge, rebuke, guidance, inspiration and sometimes questions and doubts, but the overall effect has been to condition all my thinking with the broad tenor of the God-given Word. The Bible is a book of spiritual principles, and it is a grasp of the broad sweep of these principles that is important. Key verses and specialised study are of value, but it is all too easy to lose sight of the forest as a whole, while becoming too preoccupied with some of the individual branches and twigs of the trees.

Over many years I have tried to 'preach the Word', quite often based on the Scripture Union reading for the day. One overall effect of our systematic reading and teaching has been to keep many of us SU members from becoming side-tracked into some religious speciality. And what has been true of many individuals has also been true of our Scripture Union movement as a whole right across the world. Probably more than anything else it has kept our worldwide movement free from an unbalanced emphasis and from ill-conceived doctrines and cranky sideshows. Among other things it has taught us to hold fast to two great scriptural principles: the doctrines of divine sovereignty and human responsibility. As a railway engine rests firmly on the parallel railway lines, so we can base our beliefs and our actions equally on these two principles.

When I returned to Bootham for my last year it was as a fully committed Christian, and I then began to question more seriously the theologically liberal teaching which we were given in our scripture classes.

I wrote to W. G. Ovens, the first of a line of 'great' men who, as CSSM staff members, deeply influenced my life, and he sent me a long handwritten letter of advice and comment which I treasured for many years. He advised me to subscribe to the *Bible League Quarterly*, which I did, and this led to some wider reading of an apologetic nature. I also corresponded with my father on the subject and, all in all, it was a time of mental struggle and spiritual awakening. Inevitably there was a conflict between the old and the new, the conservative teaching of my home background and the academic teaching at school. I tended to lean towards the conservative, and in this I may have been influenced by a growing sense of history, in that we ought to conserve and not lightly cast off the great storehouses of wisdom and piety of the past.

I insisted to myself that I should try to face the problems honestly, and to preserve my personal integrity and follow truth wherever it might lead. But I did so cautiously. I was not an isolated individual; whichever way I went would affect the lives of others. Our school motto, *Membra summus corporis magni* (we are members of a great body), was a reminder of this. I felt it right to lean towards the people I knew best and trusted most, and not to embark too easily on abstract and, maybe, novel ideas. Perhaps I realised that I was young and had a lot to learn from older and wiser heads than my own, and the solutions to some of the problems could wait. There was no immediate hurry; an old medical dictum warns us not to be the first to accept a new idea nor the last to try it out; and unknowingly I was trying to put this into practice.

I do not remember being homesick except for one occasion when, in bed one night, I thought of my stepmother's work-worn hands. I remembered all she had done for us four, otherwise motherless, children, and I hid my head beneath the blankets and cried. I once gave her a box of chocolates. Long afterwards, my father told me that she hoarded them and made them last for weeks, only allowing herself one at a time, so precious were they. How I wish I had done it more often!

So my cherished days at Bootham drew to an end. My last school report, after some mildly complimentary remarks, added: 'But he still continues to talk when he should act.'

2 MEDICAL STUDENT

During my final year at school I had to decide what to do next. We had an excellent school Natural History Society and I became interested in studying the social insects; the ants, bees and wasps, and I had dreams of becoming an entomologist. But following my commitment to Christ at the Lochearnhead camp, I began to think of a career in medicine. It seemed to me that this would combine an interest in nature and science with the additional vocation of the relief of human suffering and perhaps missionary service. When I mentioned this to my parents they readily agreed.

So on an October morning in 1924 I became a medical student at Glasgow University. Professor (later Sir) Graham Kerr's lectures on Zoology were so influential that I was tempted to give up medicine in favour of Zoology, but having committed myself to medicine I soon dismissed the idea. Professor Kerr gave a brilliant series of lectures on evolution which greatly impressed me, for the study of the subject had moved a long way from Darwin's researches and tentative conclusions. The more men study nature the more complex their thinking becomes, and the less dogmatic and simplistic their conclusions.

My own, no doubt, over-simplified conclusion was, and on the whole still is, that it is one thing to accept evolutionary change as a working hypothesis in the physical world of living things, and quite another to apply this as an overall philosophy covering the whole of human social development. If there is a constantly 'improving' development in the world of nature, it does not necessarily follow that there is an inevitable 'upward' development in human society as is claimed by the Marxists. With them the evolutionary theory of progression towards an ultimate utopia on earth is an article of faith of quasi-religious significance. Darwin's original modest claims and suggestions were taken by Huxley and proclaimed with evangelistic fervour up and down the country. I felt that I could sympathise with

21

Darwin but not with Huxley. The socialist dream is too mechanistic and has not in fact been achieved. I have since realised that the theory of evolution is not one to be considered in isolation but is part of a wider concept to be discussed in the last chapter. During our student days this problem did not greatly worry us. There was so much to learn both from nature and Genesis that there was little need to consider them mutually exclusive. Once we became involved with clinical medicine the sorrows and sufferings of the poor and needy left little room for abstract theorising.

Before going to university I had some qualms as to the risks which might be involved in intellectual battles lying ahead, and the possible dangers of being swept into the more undesirable aspects of social life. The obvious answer was to find some Christian friends, and the search didn't last for long. Cyril Nye was a member of the same medical year and he was also a part-time tutor at the Glasgow Bible Training Institute. We quickly formed a friendship which was maintained throughout our student years: an inestimable benefit to us both. We soon discovered a small group of evangelicals who were meeting for prayer and Bible study in a noisy room in the Students' Union. A constitution had been recognised by the University Senate in February 1923, and the group was known as the Glasgow University Christian Students' Fellowship.

Its origins dated back to the spring of 1921 when three men resigned from what was then the Christian Union, and later the Student Christian Movement in Glasgow University. They formed a prayer and Bible study group of about seven members, and in the autumn of 1923 they held a public meeting with Mr. Rendle Short, the Bristol surgeon, as the speaker. Contacts were made with similar groups in Edinburgh, St. Andrews and Aberdeen and the first Scottish Inter-Varsity Conference was held over Easter, 1925.

The Christian Students' Fellowship at Glasgow continued to grow in numbers and maturity and, by February 1928, we were ready for our first five-day mission, to be conducted by Bishop Taylor Smith.

John Taylor Smith, formerly a missionary in Nigeria, Chaplain-General of the British Forces and a personal friend of Queen Victoria, had a profound influence on our group and some influence on the university as a whole. In getting his message across he had the knack of telling memorable stories and parables which stuck in one's mind for many years. He also had a keen sense of humour and his burly figure, clerical collar, episcopal apron and gaiters, marked him out for attention. He became quite popular with the students who crowded the Union debating hall to hear him speak during the lunch hour. Instead of addressing us from the rostrum he mounted the speaker's table and, with his mellow resonant voice, he had us all captive to his shrewd wit and telling anecdotes.

The last evening of the series was held in the beautiful Wellington Church on the opposite side of University Avenue. It was a dark February evening and the large church was crowded to capacity. The organist was blind, and we watched him feeling his way into the organ loft where he paused for prayer. Seldom have I heard a church organ played with such feeling. The bishop preached with power, everyone hanging on his words, and during the closing hymn the organist was so inspired that the music seemed to soar above our heads and lift us out of ourselves.

When everyone had gone, I was standing with the bishop in the vestry. I suppose I must have been looking at him with adulation and respect for he turned and, looking at me with his clear blue eyes, he said with emphasis: 'Young man, put not your trust in princes, not even in bishops.'

In the after-glow of the great meeting and in the warmth of affection which so many of us had come to feel towards him, it would have been easy for him, as a lonely bachelor, to have invited me somewhere for coffee, and we could have talked late into the night with an emotional build-up between us. But it seemed that he deliberately handed me off. I have often quoted this incident in talks to colleagues and camp officers.

During the years at the university some young men from the Gospel Hall, Kilmacolm, visited neighbouring assemblies or mission halls to conduct their services. On one occasion, we went to Port Glasgow where we had been invited to speak at a small mission hall. In those days, partly in the after-glow of the Moody and Sankey meetings, there were many such groups scattered throughout the Glasgow area and in surrounding towns. They were little foci of love and light in a grim world. The one to which we went was known as the Byre Hall. It had originally been a cow byre but had been converted into a small meeting place.

Before coming in, we held an open-air meeting outside. On several occasions, as we stood singing under the lamplight, a scraggy, half-drunken woman would stand watching us and calling out in a slurred accent, 'Shing "Jesus knows all about our troubles."'

There she would stand in the edge of the lamplight, swaying gently on her feet and beating time with her poor skinny hands as we sang to a simple haunting melody:

> Jesus knows all about our troubles,
> He will guide till the day is done.
> There's not a friend like the lowly Jesus,
> No, not one. No, not one!

As often as not, it would be raining and then her hair hung in wisps and her meagre clothing was inadequate protection. Behind her the grim background was dirty buildings, cobbled stones and the windows of the Byre Hall which had iron bars and netting, as protection against the stone-throwing and other vandalising by the local youth. We sometimes managed to persuade her to come with us into the little building where the walls were whitewashed and which had a comfortable atmosphere. Rosy-cheeked women would be pouring out cups of tea and serving buns and the contrast between outside and in was quite marked. More than one member of the congregation would be tipsy and in the cosy atmosphere, one or another would soon be asleep. We sang the Moody and Sankey hymns set to popular tunes and did our best to convey something of the message of the love of Christ.

It was out of simple beginnings such as this that some of the great social reforms took place in the last century. The splendid work of the Salvation Army and other voluntary bodies and many social and legislative reforms, to be followed later by the Welfare State, came from such activities. All too obviously the Welfare State is not the complete answer. There are, and always will be, many loopholes still waiting to be filled by men and women who are ready to care for 'the least, the last and the lost', and to show the love of Christ in practical ways.

At the other end of the social scale, on the prosperous western side of Glasgow, there were churches which were crowded on Sundays with fashionable congregations. At one of these the minister was a certain Dr. Eady. Nearby there was a mission hall in a poor area, known locally as Cambridge Street. Someone parodied the situation as follows:

> This church is not for the poor and needy,
> But for the rich and Dr. Eady.
> If rich, come in and take your seat.
> If poor, move on to Cambridge Street.

During the summer holidays, I served my apprenticeships as a beach mission worker and camp officer. The commandant of the Scottish camps for twelve years was Montague Goodman and his superb teaching at camp prayers influenced generations of campers. I can remember some of his messages to this day. Frank Millard, who had led the camp I attended as a schoolboy at Lochearnhead, coached me in the art of children's evangelism at Elie CSSM on the east coast of Scotland. I have an old photograph of a group of workers at Elie CSSM in 1903 which includes our mother, taken the year before she was married. Our children and grandchildren have attended missions and camps, five generations in all. As individuals and as a family, we owe an enormous debt to the CSSM and Scripture Union.

The programme at Elie each summer maintained a fairly uniform pattern over the years. Each mission was usually led by an experienced leader, assisted by a team of helpers. It would last from three to four weeks and was an excellent training ground for future missionaries and Christian workers.

The wide stretch of sandy beach was a vast sand tray for building castles and having tide fights, text-making competitions, rag rugger, puddox and many other wide games. There were lantern lectures in the evenings on the life of Christ, *Pilgrim's Progress* and missionary subjects, and then there was the great day of the Birthday Service. This marked the founding of the CSSM in 1867, and on this occasion a

25

large birthday cake would be cut and there would be an extra special sand pulpit, a visiting speaker and organised sports with children and parents in the afternoon, which encouraged a great family spirit.

The holiday atmosphere made it easy to make friends. As in Scripture Union camps the key was 'friendship evangelism' although we never used that phrase.

The members of the mission team were not remote from the children and their families. The games, swimming, picnics and other activities were all mixed up with beach services and evening occasions. All this, as R. T. Archibald reminded us, was very unlike the remote preacher who depended too much on his sermons and lived remotely from his people:

> The parish priest of austerity climbed up
>   the high church steeple
> To be nearer God so that he might
>   Hand down His word to the people.
> In sermon script he daily wrote
>   What he thought was sent from heaven,
> And he dropped it down on the people's heads
>   Two times, one day in seven.
> In his age, God said, 'Come down and die!'
>   And he cried out from the steeple,
> 'Where art Thou Lord?' and the Lord replied
>   *Down here among my people.*

It was probably also R. T. Archibald who coined the phrase that we have to 'earn the right to speak' to someone else by the road of personal friendship. He warned that much harm can be done by over-zealous pressure. 'We all know of cases,' he said, 'where God was gently unfolding a young life, and someone presumed to tear open the bud, with disastrous consequences. The Lord never tore scales from the eyes.' I was taught then, and believe now, that the keynote must always be *respect* for the personality of the child or adult. Jesus loved people and loved their company, whether or not the opportunity to preach to them was there.

One of our earliest members of the Glasgow University Christian Students' Fellowship was a quiet young man from

Renfrew, William Barclay. We little thought that in later years he would become one of the most famous and popular theologians in the world, the author of more than sixty books. His *Daily Study Bible* sold some five million copies. As with J. H. Oldham, he turned his deafness to good account, in that he could shut himself off from the outside world and concentrate all the more on his scholarly pursuits. In a letter written shortly before he died he wrote, 'I have no hesitation whatever in saying that I will be glad if you will quote me as being one of the original number.' He added that ties with the Fellowship grew looser as those with the Faculty of Divinity grew stronger.

Towards the end of my student days the effects of the world-wide economic depression became increasingly severe. About this time my father's business collapsed. He had built a number of terraced houses in the south side of Glasgow on the strength of a large loan from the bank. These houses were now almost unsaleable. He was desperately worried and haunted by the fear of bankruptcy. I came home one day and found my mother in the kitchen. She said, 'Your father is in the drawing room, go in and see him.' I found him in an armchair by the fire looking haggard and hollow-cheeked. He had had some kind of nervous breakdown resulting from strain, so I took him away for a short holiday to recuperate. It was mid-winter and one night I set off on my own to climb the hills behind Largs. The ground was covered with snow and the stars clear and bright. There was a marvellous moonlit view of the Firth of Clyde and the lights of Largs far below. As I stood there, worried and perplexed, an old phrase rang through my mind: 'Follow thy star, and let not the vision glorious fade from thine eyes.' It was one of a number of hilltop experiences which, coming at a time of anxiety, were to refresh the spirit and give renewal of hope and courage to face the future. My father gradually recovered and so did his business affairs.

When we came to the study of clinical medicine in our final year, I was fortunate to be included in a small group taught by Dr. Douglas Russell at the Victoria Infirmary on the south side of Glasgow.

About a dozen of us, the number was kept deliberately small, would sit in a semicircle facing a patient in a wheelchair. Dr. Russell would begin with the student next to him, and ask what he saw as he studied the appearance of the patient. Comments would be made: the whiteness of the hair, the texture of the skin, some asymmetry of the face, the droop of the shoulder, and so on. Each student, in turn, would make his observations, hoping to spot something which the others had missed. Then, Dr. Russell would tell us what he saw, and we were astonished that we had missed so much.

We were drilled in the fourfold rule of diagnosis; inspection, palpation, percussion and auscultation, looking, feeling, tapping, and listening. The latter, incidentally, might have been with or without the aid of a stethoscope. So we each reported on what we saw, felt, percussed and heard and Dr. Russell would then sum up; the hour flew by in no time.

Modern technological aids in diagnosis are far in advance of the simple drill just described, yet there is no ultimate substitute for an elementary training in incisive observations of the whole person. The patient is a human being, full of emotions and personal values, not merely an object or case to be investigated by the technicians. In these discussions James Russell was always careful to ensure that nothing was said which would cause distress; in fact by getting the patient's consent, it often happened that he enjoyed the seminar as much as we did.

During the last few years of study and clinical work, it became necessary to concentrate on completing the course and passing the final exams. This meant less time for more specific Christian activities. It was a fascinating time, as we were given an opportunity to gain experience in one speciality after another. But it was also a time of 'scorning delights and living laborious days . . .'

Eventually the final results were posted on a pillar near the main entrance. I could hardly believe my eyes when I saw my name among the passes. In a daze I walked down the hill for the last time.

There followed almost immediately an interesting job as a house surgeon at the Victoria Infirmary at a salary of ten shillings a week. It was a teaching hospital with a fine tradition and capable consultants.

As in all hospitals, the Victoria Infirmary had the usual mixture of heartbreak and joy, but it had its humorous side too. During a ward round, I came across a cot containing a small boy. I learned that he came from a remote corner of the Highlands. With my pen at the ready, I asked,

'What's your name, laddie?'

In a soft drawl, he replied, 'Angus MacDonald'.

'What's your address?'

'Eh?'

'What's your address?'

'Eh?'

'Where do you live?'

With a surprised little smile at my ignorance, he answered, 'A wee bit past the shop.'

Another not so humorous incident stands out, which shows how easy it is to be influenced by the way someone else looks at things. One night a young man was brought in with severe damage to his hand, a motor-bike casualty. He seemed strangely free from pain and treated his injury lightly. His casual attitude spread to me and I stitched him up in a rough and ready way, without an anaesthetic. He didn't wince or seem to mind and off he went. Within the next day or two he returned as an outpatient. I found my chief, assisted by sister, ruefully surveying my crude first-aid. He said not a word, but the look he gave me is etched on my memory to this day.

So I learned two lessons on that day. Firstly, that one must not be deceived by the casual attitude of a patient, but must assess the full implications of the condition and treat it with the seriousness it deserves. The other was that my clumsy attempt at surgical first-aid had reinforced my desire to be a physician rather than a surgeon.

One winter's night, a few of us were sitting round the fire in the doctors' sitting room. We had all been medical students together over the last five years and so we knew each other fairly well. The talk turned to religion, and after some general discussion, one of my colleagues said, 'John, you've been with us all these years and you've had no more influence on us than this mantelpiece has,' and he struck the upright of the mantelpiece with the back of his hand. It was a knockout blow. Andrew Tindal who, as far as I knew, was not a Christian, jumped quickly to my defence as he saw how hurt I was. But I suddenly realised that I had spent so much time in trying to build up the 'saints' that I had cut myself off, all too much, from the 'sinners'.

This is our perennial problem as Christians. How to live in two worlds at once: the cosy world of Christian fellowship, and the other world of ordinary human beings with their problems and joys. How to follow the narrow way with our brothers and sisters in Christ and, at the same time, have real friendships with our fellow men without compromise; I have not yet found the answer. I wish I had.

One evening I was called downstairs to see a child and was accompanied by one of our consultants. The child had a skin rash and an acute ear infection. When we had completed our diagnosis, I asked the consultant to have a look at a skin rash on my own chest. He asked to see my throat. It was red and swollen. 'You've got scarlet fever,' he reported, 'well and truly.' My colleagues pelted the ambulance with snowballs as I was taken off to the Belvedere Fever Hospital. Here I was immured in a single room off one of the main wards and told that I must stay quietly in bed for six weeks as a heart murmur had developed. Reviewing the situation, I came to realise that the pressure of work during the final year of study and then at the hospital had resulted in a loss of spiritual life. There had been a time of fairly serious doubts and questioning which had been left unresolved and had inhibited spiritual growth and vitality. Lying quietly in bed, I came to see this as a God-given opportunity to sort things out, both spiritually and intellectually. I made up my mind that for the first fortnight in my hospital room I would set myself a course of Bible reading, to the temporary exclusion of other books.

The effect was remarkable. I gradually came to feel as if I was climbing a spiritual mountainside. It was not possible to work fully through the various problems and doubts, but these fell into their proper place and seemed to sort themselves out as, in imagination, I continued to climb. The long-distance perspective came into view and thoughts and plans began to emerge for a future life of service. There is an old saying, 'Beware of the barrenness of a busy life.' I believe that in the goodness of God I had been rescued from this barrenness by the enforced period of solitude and meditation. This was to serve, in the coming years, as an important principle, emphasising the need to retreat from time to time in order to regain perspective.

It was not long before I discovered that the sister in charge was a Christian. She was very interested to hear my account of the growth and development of the Glasgow University Christian Students' Fellowship and we talked about the possibility of a similar development among nurses.

Thirty-three years later I was to receive the following letter from the Rev. D. Nairn of Thurso in Caithness:

Dear Dr. Laird,

I thought you might be interested to know that the other day my wife and I had over to tea from Brough, Dunnet, a Miss Marie Wilson and a friend from Glasgow.

During our conversation, Miss Wilson recalled that it was when you were a patient in the ward of which she was sister in Belvedere Hospital that the Nurses' Christian Fellowship was really first formed and that you were its inspiration!

Today we see in the China Inland Mission prayer calendar that someone had been appointed president of the NCF in Malaya! 'See how great a forest a tiny spark can set ablaze'! (James 3.5: Amplified New Testament).

My heart murmur gradually cleared up, but cardiac discomfort, in one form or another, has never been far away. Much later, in July 1969, an acute heart attack would threaten my life.

My next job was a house physician at the Western Infirmary in Glasgow, which was a great teaching hospital near to the University. It was superbly organised under the benign dictatorship of Colonel McIntosh whose ruddy cheeks and military moustache were a familiar sight in the hospital corridors. I felt at home at once, as I had happy memories of classes as a student. I had been the clinical clerk of my chief, James Carslaw, who headed a small team of expert clinicians. In those days we were paid no salary; we had our accommodation and our meals and that was that. But, even so, there was still competition for the jobs.

One of my first patients was a frail old lady who had been sent to us because her GP was unable to locate the cause of

31

her illness. I set to work and wrote my report, diagnosing a deep-seated abdominal cancer. When Dr. Carslaw read it he seemed very pleased with my conclusions, and this diagnostic success reinforced a growing conviction that medicine, not surgery, would be my eventual choice.

The out-patients of the Western Infirmary, as in all great hospitals, provided an interesting study in human nature. One never knew what would happen next.

One afternoon I was called to see a woman in a side room. She had a friend with her and she complained of a minor skin condition just below the left clavicle, close to the neckline of her dress. No sooner had I started to examine it than she pulled up her dress round her neck quite unnecessarily, to let me examine her complaint. She had no underclothes on. Her poor, skinny body presented no temptation though, all too obviously, that had been her intention. I cleared out sharply and sent in the first nurse I could find. What happened about her skin condition I never knew. I think I acted rightly, all things considered; I cannot see how I could have done otherwise at that particular moment. But the experience opened a door of insight and compassion for the tragic lives of the street women of our cities.

Yet in my medical student days in the poorest slums of Glasgow I vividly remember that many of these tenement flats were well cared for. On one occasion I delivered a mother in the old box bed and, when tidying up afterwards, found an older child asleep at the bottom of the bed. Where else could she sleep? It was the only bed in the house. Yet in spite of the poverty the little tenement flat was clean and tidy and the family seemed united and happy.

3 NEW DIRECTIONS

During the university years, there wasn't much time to think of the future, but after graduating and gaining hospital experience, plans had to be considered.

China was often in my thoughts, with the possibility of offering to the China Inland Mission (now the Overseas Missionary Fellowship) and I was also considering working in China with Brethren missionaries. Consequently, I wrote to Professor Rendle Short of Bristol who was the professor of surgery there, a much respected leader in Brethren Assemblies and also in the student world. His reply in precise and tiny handwriting was characteristic.

> Dear Laird,
> I see no scriptural reason why you should go to China,
> 1 With the CIM
> 2 With the Brethren
> 3 Or stay at home
> > Yours sincerely,
> > (signed) A. Rendle Short

But there was a complicating factor. My father's architectural practice and building programme had not fully recovered, and my three younger sisters, Mona, Martha and Nancy, had years of study ahead of them in university education and nursing and there were no government grants in those days. My own medical education had been expensive and it therefore seemed only right to stand by the family.

There was, however, a possible alternative. Why not get a well paid medical job in one of the Chinese seaport cities to cover the next few years, after which missionary work in inland China could be considered?

About this time, an advertisement appeared in the *British Medical Journal* for a second assistant commissioner for public health for the city of Shanghai at 650 taels a month. It appeared

33

to be a responsible job, largely relating to administration and public health, in neither of which I had any special experience. To my surprise, I was called to London for an interview, at which I was told that my application was successful, subject to a satisfactory medical report. However, X-rays showed evidence of latent pulmonary tuberculosis which would probably be activated under the conditions prevailing in Shanghai.

So there I was in London without a job. I made my way to the nearest church, St. Clement Danes in the Strand, and in a quiet corner thought and prayed. Then I remembered that some time previously my friend, Tom Murray, who had been a medical colleague in the Glasgow Western Infirmary, had been offered a job as a ship's surgeon on a cadet training ship. He had been unable to accept, but had offered to suggest me as his substitute. It had been an attractive offer but I could not accept as my chief was on holiday at the time and I had still some weeks to go to finish my contract with the hospital.

I might have been able to wangle it by arrangement with the superintendent in Dr. Carslaw's absence, but he had been a good chief to me, and, in any case, I could not think of letting him down, even for a short period. Later, Dr. Carslaw's parting injunction had been, 'Don't waste a perfectly good medical education on missionary work.' I appreciated his well-meant and kindly thought, but inwardly, on this occasion at least, I begged to differ.

The memory of all this came back to me as I sat in the quiet church with London's traffic roaring outside. Here I was in London; what better place to find a job as a ship's surgeon? And why not find a ship going to the China ports? One could, at least, visit them briefly. And again, what better than a long sea voyage for an improvement in health?

I set off at once to the head offices of one big shipping company after another, but nothing doing. One smart lift-boy condescendingly told me that his company only accepted surgeons who had been qualified for at least five years; it was all somewhat disheartening.

A cup of tea in a Lyons tea shop did not quite have the atmosphere of St. Clement Danes; but, as the hymn puts it, 'Where'er they seek thee, thou art found, and every place is hallowed ground.' So here again, prayer was made for guidance. It was now late afternoon. The sensible thing was surely to catch the night train back to Scotland and think again. So off I went down Leadenhall Street on my way to the nearest Underground station. Then something happened which, in the next twenty minutes, was to alter the entire course of my life.

I found myself passing an inconspicuous door marked 122 and, glancing up, saw the following words over the door: The New Zealand Shipping Company. I could see no reason why I should not have one last try, so in I went.

'Do you happen to have a vacancy for a ship's surgeon?' I asked.

The man looked at me in surprise.

'As a matter of fact we have; we had a telegram an hour ago from one of our ship's doctors, cancelling his appointment. Would you be interested in the vacancy?'

He then told me that the ship was the SS *Northumberland*; that she was a cadet training ship, and that the ship's doctor would be expected to care, not only for the physical welfare of the cadets, but for their moral welfare as well. The divinely-given jigsaw was fitting into place, the only snag being that New Zealand wasn't China. But a sea voyage to New Zealand and back was surely ideal health-wise, and the salary being quite good it would be easy to save some money to help the family at home if necessary.

I promised to give my reply the next day, and went off, marvelling at these things and caught the night train back to Glasgow. My father and stepmother were whole-heartedly in favour, and ten days later the *Northumberland* sailed down the Clyde for Liverpool and New Zealand with me on board.

On November 8th, promptly at eleven thirty a.m., the gangway was lifted at North Sandon Dock, Liverpool. The tugs began to toot and churn up the water, even though there was still some cargo lying on the dock. The stevedores were slinging crates aboard until there was quite a broad lane of water between us and the wharf but we could not wait or we would have missed the tide. 'Old Deacon', the pilot, told us many a tale of his exploits and experiences in days gone by as we hove to, waiting till the hatches were firmly secured and the big crane dismantled and fastened to the port scuppers with wire hawsers and bolts. Half an hour later we stood out to sea. All around us the sea was dotted with big and little ships and a magnificent Canadian Pacific liner, very dignified in white paint, was being escorted by her cheeky fore-and-aft tugs. Near to us there was a fruit boat from the Mediterranean and a packet-steamer en route for Ireland.

About six p.m. the sun set gloriously behind Anglesey and when its red rays finally disappeared, all that remained to be seen of Britain was the steady flash of light from the Skerries Lighthouse, the dark line of land and the low, misty clouds.

Reflecting later on these events, I realised that it was no mere chance that I had happened to glance up at that particular moment at the offices of the New Zealand Shipping Company. If I had reached that doorway half an hour later the office would have been closed; or if that telegram had arrived an hour later I would never have gone to New Zealand. In all probability I would have returned to Glasgow and, as the door to China seemed closed, would have followed an orthodox medical career and never met the woman who would become my wife. I little thought, as I prayed in St. Clement Danes Church and in the Lyons tea shop, that people on the other side of the world were praying just then for someone to come and help them. It is strange that some of our biggest decisions and turning points in life seem to happen almost in a flash, while others are the fruit of long deliberation and heart-searching, but one God is Lord of them all.

Captain Upton had offered to alert me if anything interesting happened during the voyage, so I was not surprised when a knock came at my cabin door.

'Excuse me, sir, are you awake?'

'Yes — what is it?'

'The captain sends you his compliments, sir, and we are within a quarter of an hour of the mole at Colon.'

'All right, thanks.'

I sat up in my bunk and looked at the time; just after midnight. Pulling on a jacket and trousers over my pyjamas, I made my way to the bridge.

The Panama Canal at last: for the next hour the ship moved at dead slow, guided only by a system of lights from the shore, green, red and white; some steady, some winking out and in at intervals of so many seconds, some stationary and some moving to and fro at the mast heads of lightships. There was no sound, except now and then the voice of one of the apprentices calling the depths in fathoms as he swung the lead. Once a message flashed out from the darkness in Morse code and was answered by dots and dashes of light from our ship.

It was a warm tropical night, the sea completely calm. As my eyes grew accustomed to the darkness, I could see the low-lying coast of Central America with an occasional palm tree silhouetted on the skyline. Immediately ahead was the entrance to the harbour of Colon, at the Atlantic end of the Canal. The harbour was enclosed between two great concrete moles except for the gap towards which we were moving. It seemed a very narrow gap to me, and I thought, 'A tricky bit of navigation here. The old man must have put one of his most experienced quartermasters on the wheel tonight.'

But to my surprise, as I looked into the wheel-house, I saw by the dim light of the binnacle, the slim figure of Ennever, a boy of seventeen, at the wheel. 'The old man must be mad,' I thought, 'to entrust to a lad the steering of this great ship through such a narrow entrance. The slightest deviation would grind her hull against the concrete.' Then I saw, standing in the shadows beside the boy, the tall figure of the American pilot. I could hear his quiet orders: 'Two points to the starboard, four points to the starboard, steady, bring her round' and so the *Northumberland*, with over ninety men on board, many of them asleep, slipped quietly into the harbour.

At five a.m. on December 17th, 1930, I watched the sun rising over New Zealand. It was a magnificent sight. The volcanic character of the country was very apparent, jagged lava cliffs, needles of rock and tiny unexpected islands. The golden sheen of the early sunshine pervaded everything. A fresh breeze made white horses all around; seagulls circled above and a few dolphins swam alongside.

By ten a.m. we were tied up at the wharf in Auckland. My first impressions surprised me. I could hardly believe that having travelled over 12,000 miles from England, I was not back there again. The streets were crowded with English-speaking people who looked, dressed and spoke very much the same as one would have found in one of the smaller English cities. Threading my way through the crowds on this warm summer morning, I overheard a young mother say to her child, 'If we hadn't won the war the Germans would have been here!' I almost imagined I was dreaming and I was back in England after all!

Before leaving home I had paid a visit to Pickering and Inglis' bookshop in Glasgow. When I told Cecil Pickering that I was about to set off for New Zealand, he suggested that if ever I was in Auckland I might call on a Mr. Thatcher, a former member of his staff, and now manager of a bookshop in Upper Symonds Street, Auckland.

So it seemed natural to make my way through the streets until I found the bookshop and met Mr. Thatcher himself. After some general conversation, I asked him if he knew anything about the activities of the CSSM and Scripture Union to which he replied that he didn't.

At this juncture, Mr. Arthur Tucker came into the shop and Mr. Thatcher introduced me to him. He told me that CSSM activities were just beginning in New Zealand. During the previous summer a beach mission had been held for the first time, and now a second mission was about to begin at Brown's Bay, not far from Auckland. His future son-in-law might like to meet me as he was going to be the leader of the first CSSM boys' camp in New Zealand, the one at Brown's Bay. His name was Howard Knight and arrangements were made for us to meet the following day. Mr. Thatcher then telephoned Dr. Pettit who, he said, was interested in the kind of work we were discussing, and within an hour I was in Dr. Pettit's home.

Dr. Pettit was a slim, alert, intelligent man, aged about 45, who expressed himself clearly and logically and with a ready sense of humour. On the mantelpiece was a photograph of Howard Guinness and our conversation immediately turned to Howard's recent whirlwind visit to New Zealand.

After graduating in medicine in 1928, Howard had been appointed travelling secretary of the infant Inter-Varsity Fellowship. In that year he went to Canada, then on to Australia and, through Dr. Pettit's advocacy, had arrived in New Zealand in October 1930. Some evangelical students had already begun to meet in Auckland in February 1927,

38

but they were a small group who, to use their own phrase, had 'plodded on quietly'. With the coming of Howard Guinness, the movement sprang into life.

From Auckland, Howard travelled throughout the dominion, speaking at school assemblies and forming enthusiastic Christian groups in schools and university colleges. Without consulting the Crusaders' Union in England, he decided to call these groups 'Crusaders' and suggested that they should have the same badge as the former which later led to difficulties and complications. Eventually the name Crusaders was dropped in New Zealand and these school groups are now known as the Inter-School Christian Fellowship.

At the end of this two-month inspirational tour, Howard returned to Australia, leaving a rejoicing but slightly bewildered committee, with a new organisation on their hands and very little knowledge or experience to guide them as to what to do next. This was the group who had been praying that the Lord would send someone with experience to follow the splendid initiative which Howard Guinness had created, just at the time when I was praying for guidance in London.

Meantime, Dr. Pettit himself had been so concerned about the need for follow-up, that he had considered relinquishing his practice for a time and visiting some schools himself. However, he had been quite unable to get a locum to look after his practice. For my part, I was able to tell him of the rapid development of evangelical activities at my own university and many others throughout Britain.

He there and then suggested that I should leave my ship, take over his practice for six months and set him free to make a tour of the schools and colleges. I replied that I had signed on for the round trip and could not break my contract. It appeared, however, that there would be little difficulty in finding a New Zealand doctor to take my place for the return voyage. I returned to the ship late that evening somewhat dazed at the extraordinarily rapid turn of events.

Next day, I met Howard Knight, who was full of plans for his boys' camp at Brown's Bay. I also met a number of student leaders, and on the only Sunday in port, I spoke at a boy's Bible class in a Baptist Church. Among them was Colin Becroft of whom we shall hear later.

Our ship was on the New Zealand coast for some months, first unloading and then reloading before returning to England. During this time I met many people who later became intimate friends and colleagues. They included Dr. and Mrs. Gordon Anderson in Wellington, Mr. and Mrs. Fountain in Christchurch and the Rev. and Mrs. Basil Taylor and their family. I found that Basil Taylor's mother had been one of the early SU secretaries in New Zealand in the last century and that he was, at that time, the New Zealand honorary secretary.

But meantime, something was about to happen which drove all thoughts from my mind, for I became involved in a major disaster.

I was about to knock at the captain's cabin door to ask permission to go ashore to have tea with some of my newly-made friends, when suddenly the ship began to shudder violently. It was a warm February morning in 1931 and our ship, the *Northumberland*, was lying in the roadstead off the town of Napier on the east coast of the north island of New Zealand.

Looking ashore we saw the whole of the big cliff face rolling down into the sea, sending billows of yellow dust high into the sunlit air. The bosun's first reaction was to look aloft at the rigging. The captain at once made for the bridge and put the engine-room at the 'stand by' and the stevedores came tumbling up from the holds and started shouting that they must be allowed on shore. The head stevedore was wringing his hands and running distractedly about as he thought he had seen his house falling down the cliff face. It turned out later, however, that his home and family were safe.

In a few minutes they were all aboard the lighters and making for the shore and we were left on the ship. Our chief engineer was below at the time and he thought that the whole engine-room was about to break up around him. Our ship had been hit either directly by the sudden rising of the sea bottom, or the earthquake may have been transmitted through the water to the ship's keel. There was no wharf deep enough to take us so we were lying well out in the shallow bay.

A message was given over the radio that doctors and nurses were urgently needed so permission was quickly given to go ashore and I with a small group of helpers set off in one of the ship's lifeboats, taking such medical equipment as we had available. The wind had risen and the sea had become choppy.

One of our rescue team was Mahoney, a ship's steward. Each evening at sea, Mahoney would bring me a hot drink at bedtime and we had many a yarn on these occasions, often on the subject of religion. Mahoney was a nominal Roman Catholic and I think he probably came to a personal faith in Christ. On our way across the harbour he sat with his head in his hands. 'Are you sick, Mahoney?' I shouted. He looked up from his cupped hands and replied, 'No, sir, I'm praying.'

We tried to make our way into the inner harbour but it was impossible and so we had to land at the nearest rocks. We passed close under a big fire. Volumes of smoke were drifting across, and the fire was crackling fiercely. The two orderlies and I left the accident boat in charge of the third officer and we scrambled over the rocks to a road. The road surface was split and there were many long cracks, sometimes several feet wide.

In a few minutes we came to a wharf where a small warship, the sloop HMS *Veronica*, had tied up about fifteen minutes before the first earthquake shock. I reported to the captain immediately and was told to proceed either to the hospital or the cathedral, so we made for the hospital in a small Ford van. On the way we saw big warehouses lying in heaps with bales of wool scattered over the road. Masses of concrete lay about, and huge cracks were seen in the streets. Telegraph poles stood at rakish angles and leaned against houses and the telegraph wires were strewn wildly. We met one man who seemed mentally deranged, and many family groups were sitting helplessly on the kerbs in front of their ruined homes. The root of a big tree and a huge boulder lay in the middle of the road and in one place we saw a dead horse. In a few minutes we arrived at our destination.

The hospital and the nurses' home were in ruins. The nurses' home had collapsed like a pack of cards and many of the night nurses were killed. The adjoining gardens and a cemetery were crowded with beds and blankets, and temporary operating tents were being erected. One of the hospital buildings had been built by a builder whose shoddy work the earthquake had revealed. Concrete, which was supposed to be reinforced, had been skimped, and the evidence was etched starkly against the skyline. It seemed a vivid illustration of the apostle Paul's warning that 'the work that each man does will at last be brought to light; the day of judgement will expose it.' (1 Cor. 3:13.)

Although the hospital was in complete confusion the matron was not. There she was, immaculate in starched uniform like a ship in full sail: cool, calm and collected. She was accompanied by an assistant and seemed in complete charge of the situation.

I gratefully sought her advice and she directed us to the racecourse where the space under the grandstand had been converted into a casualty station. But before leaving the hospital grounds, I found among the wounded the lady who would have been my hostess at tea. She had been in the bath when the earthquake occurred. Jumping up in fear, she knocked a glass tumbler off a shelf which broke in the bath. She promptly sat on the broken glass and there, by the roadside, I had to suture the wound.

I heard afterwards of Miss Kate Williams, a splendid old lady of over eighty and one of the main Scripture Union honorary secretaries in New Zealand. She was at a communion service when the earthquake occurred. Her frail old hand was pinned to the communion rail by a fallen beam. When they came to release her she insisted, although in great pain, that others be helped first. She died some weeks later.

Mahoney and I commandeered a passing car, and with some difficulty we reached the racecourse and started work, Mahoney as stretcher bearer and me as first-aider. The ground was trembling beneath us from time to time. When it got dark a number of cars were arranged in a semi-circle with their headlights converging and in the pool of light we did what we could for the wounded.

In some cases all we could do was a minimum of first-aid and the relieving of pain. One old man, a cook from one of the hotels, was given a shot of morphia and space to lie down in a hastily-erected tent, a women's tent as it happened. When he awoke in the morning, surrounded by numerous ladies, he surveyed the scene with a broad grin and announced, 'Solomon in all his glory'.

We were much saddened as we sailed from Napier, leaving behind the ruined city where 256 people had been killed and many more had been injured. When we reached the open sea our men were mustered on deck where Captain Upton made a short speech of thanks and appreciation to his men. Later the Navy League presented our ship with a bronze plaque in appreciation of the help we had given.

Our next port of call was Wellington where I had already spent a short time, and it was there that I really had to take stock. I left the ship one morning and climbed one of the steep hills above the city. It was a lovely summer's day and there was a magnificent view across the great land-locked harbour and the busy seaport town.

The day was spent in waiting upon God in prayer and I believe it was there that the decision was taken to leave the ship and spend six months helping forward the work of the Crusaders and CSSM in New Zealand. This plan nearly fell through because of unexpected difficulties in finding a doctor to take my place on the homeward voyage. Once again the future hung by a single thread. At last a substitute was found just before the ship's departure from New Zealand, and a few days later I went down the ship's side carrying my suitcases, having said farewell to my fellow officers, cadets and crew whose company had been so enjoyable on the long journey. It would seem that in those days there was no need to obtain an entrance permit. It did not occur to me to enquire whether the New Zealand government would accept me as one of her citizens. I simply went ashore and was welcomed into the home of Dr. and Mrs. Gordon Anderson.

Our Scripture Union readings on the morning when I left the ship included Luke 9:61, 62; 'I will follow you, Lord; but let me first say farewell to those at my home. Jesus said to him, "No one who puts his hand to the plough and looks back is fit for the kingdom of God",' and Luke 10:2; 'The harvest is plentiful, but the labourers are few; pray therefore the Lord of the harvest to send out labourers into his harvest. Go your way; behold I send you . . .'

The next few days were somewhat of an anti-climax, as I did not quite know what to do next. Some interesting contacts were made with new friends in Wellington, but arrangements with Dr. Pettit were not yet clarified, so early one wet and dismal morning, feeling puzzled and unsure of myself, I put through a long-distance telephone call from Wellington post office to Dr. Pettit in Auckland. We discussed future arrangements, and it was finally confirmed that I would undertake the job of visiting the schools and colleges myself, and that he would continue in his practice. In effect this meant that he would then be responsible to raise the necessary money and would ensure that the Auckland committee would function. Dr. Anderson suggested that I should make a start at Nelson and within the next few days I was off on my first assignment.

4 FIRST STEPS IN NEW ZEALAND

My work in New Zealand was about to begin, and it was certainly a course of events which had never been anticipated. It was surely no mere chance that Arthur Tucker came into Thatcher's bookshop at the precise moment when he did, but for this accurate timing I might never have met Dr. Pettit and would probably have returned to Scotland as surgeon on the *Northumberland*. Archbishop Temple is reported as saying, in effect, 'When people stop praying, coincidences stop.' In my experience. the words can also be reversed: 'When people keep on praying, "coincidences" become significant'.

When I reached Alex Bain's home in Nelson, I found a letter from Dr. Pettit with the suggestion that I should stay in the South Island and go on to Christchurch and Canterbury College. As I waited on the verandah for breakfast I found myself within arm's length of ripe fruit trees and vines of various kinds. All these impressions and the friendliness of the people warmed my heart.

The college was close by and I was soon on the platform of the assembly hall. Behind me, as I spoke, was the school's honours roll, which included the names of Lord Rutherford, the famous physicist, and my friend, William H. Pettit. It seemed that his long shadow, or should I say, his shining light, was quite inescapable!

I was deeply impressed by the scene before me. Used to English schoolboys in long trousers, school uniforms and collars and ties, I was confronted with quite a contrast. Here were rows of boys of splendid physique dressed in shorts, open-necked grey shirts, with stockings and shoes suitable for the mild Nelson climate. I could see at once the tremendous potential for the future in these young people.

Next day I addressed some seventy members of the Girls' High School Christian Union and was again impressed by their freshness and potential. These few days in Nelson brought with them confirmation and courage for my new task. During the next six months I must have spoken to some seven or eight thousand boys and girls in school assemblies and small groups.

By way of illustration, I often told the story of the earthquake which had been widely reported in the press, and the story of Ennever steering the *Northumberland* into the harbour at Colon through the darkness of a tropical night. I urged them to have the Christ-Pilot standing in the shadows beside them to help them to steer the ship of their lives through stormy seas and hidden depths, using the well-tried chart of Biblical teaching, the compass of conscience, together with the leadership of Christ, to guide them and their shipmates into the harbour at the end of the voyage.

The talks given at these school assemblies were short and to the point. Stories and parables which I remembered from the days of Bishop Taylor Smith were ideally suited. For example, there was the story of the candle . . .

When the bishop was chaplain-general of the army, he was travelling by troopship. Walking on deck, he was approached by a member of the crew, who warned him that it was about to rain heavily as a storm was blowing up and that he should take cover. He made his way to the officers' smoke room, opened the door and stepped in. The room was full of men relaxing over their pipes and beer. They looked up as the door opened. A discussion had been in progress which suddenly stopped as the chaplain-general's burly figure appeared. After a moment's pause an officer said, 'Sir, may we ask you a question? We have been discussing why it should be that if God gives to men powerful desires and impulses and men gratify them, why should they then be punished for it?'

The chaplain-general was standing with his back to the door through which he had just entered. As the men looked up waiting for an answer, he lifted his heart in a brief prayer for wisdom, and as he did so he felt the pressure of the door on his back as someone tried to open it. Then a hand appeared carrying a small storm lantern which was deposited on the deck at the bishop's feet and the door was closed against the storm outside.

Suddenly the answer came. He picked up the lantern, opened it and took out the candle. Holding it up, he pointed out that there were three elements to it, the wax, the wick and the flame, the wax subordinate to the wick (to be compared to the body), with the wick running through it and emerging above it (the mind), and the flame supplied by both and superior to both. So long as the lighted candle was held upright and lit, it was fulfilling the purpose for which it had been made. But if it was turned upside down and the wax, representing the body, was given first place, above the level of the wick and flame (the spiritual part), then the flame would go out and the wax would be blackened and distorted. Consequently there would be a black mark on the deck and a somewhat unpleasant smell: a vivid illustration of the man who gives himself over to a materialistic way of life and so quenches the flame of the spirit.

After my talk at Nelson College school assembly, a group of boys met in a small upstairs room to plan their witness as a Crusader group in the school. In the next few years from one end of New Zealand to the other, there were similar groups of boys and girls meeting in lunch hours or after school for mutual encouragement, Bible study and prayer, perhaps above all, for witness. As time went on adult leaders or senior advisers were appointed to help these little groups of Christians, either members of the school staff, or carefully selected friends.

Some groups flourished, others did not. Sometimes the groups became inward-looking and unduly pious, cut off from the main-stream of the school's life. To counteract this a threefold slogan was invented. They were encouraged to witness by the quality of their scholarship, sportsmanship and school citizenship, and many of them did just that.

These were still the days of Newman's Service Cars, successors of the older horse coaches. They were powerfully built and could take from six to a dozen or more passengers with luggage, and the Royal Mail. They left Nelson Coaching Station first thing in the morning, their dark red paint freshly washed, pools of water still on the garage floor. The drivers were experienced men. The roads were gravelled and dusty, often corrugated for long stretches, and had to be constantly 'graded'. The morning newspapers were delivered at speed, the driver flicking them with unerring skill into the gateways on both sides of the road, and when these were on the left, he flicked them over the roof of the car. On one long stretch of road a farmer and his dog were standing by the gate. As the service car approached at a signal from the farmer the dog leaped forward towards us. Into the air went the tightly-rolled newspaper, to be caught in mid-air by the dog, who then raced back to his master. The end of the journey brought me to Christchurch and the love and friendship of the Fountain family.

I cycled in the early morning through the peaceful tree-lined streets of this very 'English' city, still wet after the night's rain, to meet with a small group of students, some of whom had been converted through the influence of Howard Guinness. They met in a room lent by Maud Herriott, lecturer in the botany department, where they were surrounded by plants and botanical specimens on the walls and benches.

Brief visits followed to schools at Ashburton, Timaru, Oamaru and so to the 'Scottish' city of Dunedin, where I was welcomed by the Cree Brown family.

Mr. Cree Brown, like Dr. Pettit in Auckland, had been fostering a small group of students and they too had been galvanised into new life following the visit of Howard Guinness. He had taught in a school of engineering at Poona in India, and was now a consultant engineer in Dunedin, where he was a leading layman in evangelical circles and much respected. His sandy hair, blue eyes, rugged features and pawkiness fitted in well with his Scottish ancestry, and with the classical image of the craggy Scot. When on leave from India, he proposed to pretty Kathleen Glasgow. In reply to his question 'Will you marry me and come to India with me?' she demurely replied, 'Yes please'.

Early in April 1931, some eight students and eight senior schoolboys, together with a few adults, spent five days at Karitane, a small seaside resort. The programme included Bible study and some house-to-house evangelism. Some of the eight students were already well-established Christians; others were young in the faith. From that small group three became missionaries, two Presbyterian ministers, one, Dr. Vine Martin, served for twenty-five years with the Scripture Union, and another became a banker and a leading layman in his church. Also, through the house-to-house visitation one girl was won for Christ and later became a missionary.

From then on, the days were full of school visits, various meetings, personal conversations and a children's mission at Ashburton.

On my return to Christchurch in May, I made friends with William Orange of Sumner. This remarkable man deserves a few paragraphs to himself as he played such a great part in New Zealand's evangelical history. When he was a young man in the choir of St. John's Church, Latimer Square, Christchurch, he and his fellow-choristers were processing through the church when William suddenly had a vision of Christ. He heard the Lord say to him: 'I have chosen you to be a witness to my second coming.' This made a great impression on him and undoubtedly marked his preaching in future years.

William was of slight build and quick and alert in his movements. He had an aquiline nose and the lean features of an ascetic. His expressive brown eyes, sometimes sad, sometimes lit up with irrepressible laughter, were a strong feature. He had a lovable personality yet he never married. 'I suppose I have failed to *embrace* my opportunities', he once said, half-laughingly, half-regretfully.

One day, so the story goes, on a Christchurch tram he met a Jewish rabbi who offered to teach him Hebrew. Later, at Canterbury University College, he graduated in Hebrew, Greek and philosophy and then went on to read theology at College House.

In company with a fellow student from College House who paid all expenses, he travelled for two years in many parts of the world. Whether or not he was distantly related to the royal house of Orange I cannot be sure but it is certain that when travelling in Holland, William Orange was treated with considerable respect. The experience of this tour left a deep impression on him. He missed nothing with his alert mind and keen powers of observation. He kept very detailed diaries of his travels and years later could recount incidents and conversations as if they had happened yesterday.

There is, on the waterfront at Brixham in Devon, a statue to mark the spot where William of Orange came ashore to assume the English crown. There, one can see the shortly built, well-knit figure, the aquiline nose and regular features of my friend William Orange. On a plaque below the statue are some words from a speech King William made as he came ashore: 'The Protestant religion I will maintain.'

His first charge was at Waikari in North Canterbury, a small isolated parish where he devoted himself to study, especially the book of Genesis. He was determined to find out for himself if the Genesis records were worthy of faith, for he had been taught otherwise at College. Here he laid the foundations of his extensive library of 15,000 volumes, spending his money on books rather than on a wife, as he sometimes jokingly put it. He had a good grasp of current events, with a keen sense of perception. This enabled him to size up a situation with accuracy, even in subjects far removed from his own way of life.

When I first met him he had recently become Vicar of Sumner near Christchurch. It was as if he had just come out of the wilderness where he had been with God and his books. He was aglow with the Spirit and to meet him was an inspiration.

He started a boys' Bible class and soon boys from the Crusader group at Christchurch Boys' High School and other schools were cycling down to Sumner on Sunday afternoons. On Sunday evenings the little church would be crowded as, standing on the chancel steps in his cassock and surplice, William Orange expounded the Scriptures, his warm brown eyes alight with enthusiasm. He constantly reminded us that the Bible is a book of spiritual principles and he loved the prayer of the psalmist: 'Let my prayer be set forth before thee as incense; and the lifting up of my hands as the evening sacrifice. Set a watch, O Lord, before my mouth; keep the door of my lips.' (Psalm 141:2, 3.)

His influence is felt to this day through the widespread ministry of men whom he taught and inspired, some of whom were known as 'Orange Pips'. His books are now part of the library of Latimer House, Christchurch, where they are cared for by a full-time warden. Latimer House is also a centre for Biblical and evangelical research of great value to the Christian cause in New Zealand.

When in May 1931 I suggested a small houseparty for Bible study, he readily assented. We were lent a cottage at Governor's Bay, near Christchurch, a lovely place overlooking an arm of the sea and surrounded by hills. There were ten of us and each morning we sat on the wide glassed-in verandah overlooking the bay, while William Orange would entrance us with his expositions from the book of Genesis, drawing practical lessons and stimulating us with some of the great principles of Biblical teaching. We were fascinated! It was all so fresh and new and he himself was so captivated by his theme, and so full of excitement at the spiritual treasures he had discovered that we were caught up in the warmth of his spirit. We little knew how far-reaching was to be the influence of this little group. Of the eight schoolboys, one became a missionary bishop, another a Christian headmaster, another an IVF travelling secretary and later a leading evangelical in the Church of England, another a missionary in South America and another a much-loved country vicar. They were the forerunners of many others who were to bring a new spiritual tide of evangelical warmth and enthusiasm into the churches and missionary societies of New Zealand, proving once again the value of the small group under good leadership in teaching and training future leaders. This was Jesus' own method with his twelve disciples.

Most of the year 1931 was taken up with visiting and re-visiting schools, from Whangarei in the North to Invercargill in the South, nine hundred miles from one to the other.

It soon became obvious that I could not be responsible for work among girls as well as boys, so the committee decided to appoint a woman for this important task. Margaret McGregor, M.A., formerly on the staff of Nelson Girls' College and a lecturer at the New Zealand Bible Institute, was their choice. She was appointed to the staff in September 1931, and we worked together amicably for fourteen years. She was of small build and her most memorable feature was her raven-black hair which never turned grey to her dying day. At a prayer meeting in London, Mr. Hubbard was heard to pray earnestly for Miss McGregor and Dr. Laird who were 'carrying on hand in hand in the work in New Zealand'.

Early in December I set off with a pile of books for a brief holiday at Ponui Island, some twenty-five to thirty miles from Auckland in the Hauraki Gulf. This island was owned by members of the Chamberlin family, and Fred Chamberlin and his wife, Gertie, welcomed me warmly.

I had pitched my little hike tent close to the water's edge. By ten o'clock the night was as black as pitch, but mild with no wind, and the only sounds were the lapping of the calm water on the beach and the stirring now and then of some bird or animal, while far above the Southern Cross rode the night sky. In such circumstances one could:

> 'Sense the lifting tide beneath the stars,
> And in the whispering of the waters on the sands
> Hear the still small voice of Him
> Who holds the ocean in His hands.'

My tent was pitched between two Pohutukawa trees, just coming into brilliant crimson flower. One evening I crossed the island and went part of the way on horseback, crossing the highest point from which there was a magnificent view of the rolling hills and glens of the island, flocks of sheep quietly grazing and the blue sea all around. It was an enchanting sight.

One evening, I took my kerosene lamp and went down to the beach, hung the lamp over the bow of the boat and rowed across the bay. Every dip of the oars was like fire in the calm water from the phosphorescent glow. I stopped rowing, drifted along for a bit and the fish came gathering round to the light, some leaping out of the water and some swimming around the boat, leaving a trail of fire behind them. Soon, I beached the boat, reached my tent and, after a little meditation, went off to sleep — the end of a perfect day.

Some of the best times on the island were the quiet hours when I was entirely on my own. James Russell Lowell the American poet puts it well:

If that the chosen soul
could never be alone
In deep mid-silence, open-doored to God,
No greatness ever had
been dreamed or done.
The nurse of full grown souls
is solitude.

In the years that followed, Ponui Island became one of our
first camping sites, and perhaps our best loved, where hundreds of boys and girls came to a living faith in Christ, and
where very many dedicated their lives to His service at home
and abroad.

Thus refreshed I returned to Auckland just in time for
Christmas with Mr. and Mrs. Kemp, who had become good
friends.

Joseph Kemp, minister of Auckland Baptist Tabernacle,
was a successful preacher and Bible teacher despite the fact
that he had received very little formal education, apart from
some training in the Glasgow Bible Training Institute.
Although he was no great scholar he was a very eloquent
preacher and a down-to-earth teacher. His church flourished
greatly and many of his young men grew up and made their
mark. Among the men he influenced and trained, I need
mention only two: E. M. Blaiklock and J. O. Sanders.

He showed me his library and filing system which he had
built up to compensate for his lack of scholarship. The basis of
this library and filing system was works of reference, encyclo-
pedias, dictionaries and commentaries. Added to this, he had
several filing cabinets full of pages torn from magazines,
newspaper cuttings, pamphlets and notes of current affairs,
all carefully indexed and alphabetically classified. He used
all these for his sermon material, and was thus abundantly
supplied with preacher's tools.

At once this idea clicked in my mind, and I determined to
follow his example. A little later I discovered that Oswald
Sanders had adopted a similar system which he kindly
demonstrated to me. The time came when I bought a supply
of large-sized manilla folders, each labelled with a subject.
They were then arranged alphabetically and kept in an apple

box. Later I subtracted ten pounds from my savings and bought a second-hand steel four-drawer filing cabinet, and eventually when this was full up, another cabinet.

Today the Biblical section contains sixty-six folders, one for each book of the Bible. The topical section begins with Abraham and, at the moment, ends with Worldliness! Another section contains notes of nearly every sermon or message ever given, broadly classified as Devotional, Expository, Gospel, Topical. Within each folder the notes are filed in date order, and on the front of each folder, there is a list of the contents under an appropriate title and number. This title and number is then noted at the top of each set of sermon notes. On the last page of the notes a record is made, giving the place and date when used.

The setting up of this simple system, all dating back to a Christmas Day spent with the Kemp family in Auckland, 1931, proved to be one of the most satisfying things I ever did. It has grown in value over the years and has become a sort of home-made encyclopedia and treasury. It contains extracts copied from books, poems, best thoughts, notes of addresses, lectures and sermons listened to. It also contains illustrations and stories, jokes, letters worth keeping, pictures made by children and grandchildren when they were little, and countless other things. It has the great merit of simplicity and flexibility, and personally I find it far better than a card index system, as papers of all shapes and sizes can be filed.

The mission at Brown's Bay which followed immediately, was a never-to-be-forgotten experience. We had an exceptionally gifted houseparty, among whom were Oswald and Edith Sanders, who had been married only a few weeks earlier. In later years Oswald Sanders became principal of the New Zealand Bible Training Institute, director of the Overseas Missionary Fellowship and the author of books with a circulation of over a million copies. Our friendship in the early 1930s meant much to us both and still does.

The beach services were well attended by children and their parents, the numbers increasing to some 650 on the CSSM birthday, when Oswald Sanders gave an outstanding message to the great crowd.

During this mission at Brown's Bay I had pitched my small hike tent at the far end of undeveloped land behind the house where we had our houseparty. One morning after breakfast I was visited by some small boys, obviously attracted by the tent and curious about its occupant. When small boys are around there are often dogs accompanying them, and so it was this morning. Friendly relationships were soon established, with the dogs as well as the boys, and over the next few days the visits continued. Thus it came about that the Brown's Bay dog club was established, with myself as president. We all attended as a matter of course the daily CSSM services on the beach, and soon most of the members of the dog club became members of the Scripture Union.

A problem soon arose. Some boys who did not own a dog, began to attend our very informal meetings. We were perplexed by the puzzle of how to be a member of a dog club without possessing a dog. However, someone came up with the bright idea of their becoming associate members, and the problem was resolved. Then one day the president was emboldened to suggest that, as nearly all were members of the Scripture Union, why not open the meetings with prayer, as we did at the beach services? This was somewhat tentatively agreed. But how to begin?

'The president should do it,' they agreed.

'No,' I said. 'We must all do our bit.'

'But we don't know what to say.'

Then came the brilliant suggestion that each club member should be given a slip of paper and a pencil and, with some presidential coaching, should write a short prayer. Then the prayers were put into a hat and shaken (I don't quite know why) and each boy took one and read it out when his turn came, with the proviso that the other boys, and hopefully the dogs, kept quiet. After this had gone on for several days one boy piped up, 'We don't need those bits of paper; we can pray without them.' And so they did.

What a thrill it was to be allowed to take children by the hand and lead them gently, one step at a time, into the Kingdom of Heaven. In various ways, and in all sorts of spontaneous friendships, this happened year after year at Brown's Bay and at many other beach missions and camps throughout the land. As time went on, many boys and girls quietly grew in grace, helped immensely by their daily Bible reading, school Christian Unions, and in many cases their homes and churches. In the teams of workers in later years there were many young men and women who had entered the Kingdom of Heaven with childlike trust at such beach missions.

5 CROSSROADS AND MARRIAGE

I still could not get the idea of going to China out of my head, especially as it seemed logical to find a way to make practical use of my medical training in a country like China where the need was so great.

In July 1931, Howard Mowll, at that time a missionary bishop in West China and later Archbishop of Sydney, visited New Zealand. He was a man of great administrative gifts and imaginative leadership, and consequently I was very keen to meet him, as he seemed the ideal person from whom to seek advice. In order to arrange this meeting and fit in with his very crowded programme, I discovered that he was going to travel from Auckland to Hamilton by train and, having asked his permission, I booked myself a first-class ticket and travelled with him.

The journey proved most helpful. Bishop Mowll told me that he was distressed at the lack of intellectual quality among evangelical students in England. Although he disclaimed academic distinction for himself, he said that he would do all he could to emphasise the need for an intellectual approach to the student world. He thought that although evangelical students had plenty of enthusiasm, they lacked disciplined thought and study about their faith. 'If the church is weak at home,' he said, 'and if there is no adequate source from which to draw capable and dedicated men and women recruits for the mission field, how will the battle-front fare?' He therefore urged me to remain in New Zealand, at least until a successor could be found, in order to develop a well thought-out student programme, which would include sending out missionaries with good all-round qualifications. He added that the mission field suffered because of decay at home and the wrong kind of people going out.

This discussion with Bishop Mowll did much to clarify my thinking and confirmed what was already beginning to take shape in my mind as to the 'overall strategic concept'. It was certainly worth a first-class train ticket from Auckland to Hamilton.

Towards the end of January 1932, a day was spent in fasting and prayer and I received a fresh experience of the Holy Spirit. An unmistakable glow encompassed me. I felt a touch of the Holy Spirit's power as never before and a sense of rejoicing in the Lord and in His service. People speak of 'walking on air'. I think I know what they mean, but for me I would rather compare it to the experience of Peter walking on the water to go to Jesus, and hearing His voice, 'Take heart, it is I; have no fear.'

Such experiences do not necessarily continue uninter-ruptedly. D. L. Moody was once asked if he was filled with the Holy Spirit, to which he replied, 'Yes, but I leak!'

This recognition of walking by faith was all the more pertinent at this time because there were undercurrents of deep perplexity and uncertainty as to guidance for the future. The dual awareness of joyful and fruitful service, and yet puzzlement over guidance were not inconsistent. To change the metaphor, it seemed as if something deep down was struggling to be born. Perhaps there is a sense in which we can experience other 'new births' after that essential first one, not as a 'reincarnation' in some future state, but in the world of here and now. There can be deep renewals of spiritual experience when new life and hope are born within us, a new start is made and life begins again. These mental and spiritual struggles were painful at times, but there was a strong if unexpressed confidence that out of them would come, in God's good time, the help and guidance that were needed.

It is often out of such experiences that the best guidance comes, but one must patiently await God's time, for guidance is part of the trend of a life and not merely the emotion of the moment. That which is to be born must come to maturity and not be enforced prematurely. 'If it seem slow, wait for it; it will surely come, it will not delay' (Habakkuk 2:3).

The undercurrents were pulling in three directions: the call to missionary service in China, the call of the young people of New Zealand, and the desire to go home to Scotland and continue my medical calling. But gradually thoughts and plans for future medical work began to fade and other vistas of future usefulness opened up. This was accentuated as I saw how many excellent men were at work in the healing profession. I felt that in that field I would hardly be missed, but in the world of evangelism the labourers were few indeed.

I realised increasingly, as Bishop Mowll had pointed out, that the battle lay in the realms of thought and ideas, as well as geographical location. Also if I were to go to the mission field as a single unit, this would add one individual to the missionary task force, whereas if I remained at the home base and encouraged twenty or, who knows, even fifty to go in my place, this would result in multiplication of effectiveness.

Few Christians in New Zealand at this time seemed to have grasped this concept and the significance of what was happening, and could happen, in the schools and colleges, the missionary societies and other trans-denominational agencies. Most church leaders were naturally absorbed in their local parochial work, but something more was needed: the freedom to develop new ideas and far-reaching strategies. There need be no conflict between the worshipping and caring ministry of the local church on the one hand, and the varied activities of the specialised societies on the other, for both can be manifestations of the creative activity of the same Holy Spirit.

During the years of uncertainty when I did not know in which direction to go, the sense of indecision increased the need for prayer. The early morning time for prayer and Bible reading then became increasingly important. When travelling as a guest in various homes, I often asked my hostess if she would give me breakfast on a tray in my bedroom, and usually this suited her well. This gave time for prayer, study and the preparation of messages.

> Before the multitude, before the valley,
> Before the toil that binds thee heart and hand,
> Be ready in the first fresh hour of morning
> High in the mount alone with God to stand.

From time to time I went into retreat in some quiet place for a day or two. This gave an opportunity for the ministry of intercession as there were literally hundreds to be prayed for. It also gave time to think about current problems of which there were many. The answer was not always given then and there, but quite often at least the next step would become clear. It seemed that just when needed most, fresh strength and courage and new insights would be given for the tasks ahead.

In my prayer diary on March 15th, 1929, there appear the initials 'F.' and 'M.', a private code for 'Field and Marriage'. It was a reminder to pray daily for guidance as to my future field of service and for guidance as to future marriage.

The seed thought as to 'M' had been planted years before by Bishop Taylor Smith during one of his missions at Glasgow University. Chatting informally to a group of us he said, 'Most of you men will be married some day, and the girl you are going to marry must be alive somewhere now. Why don't you start to pray for her?' To pray for someone living who would some day be my wife had never occurred to me, but the bishop's suggestion seemed a good one. But I had thought very much about the need for guidance about a future field of service. No doubt these were the two most important decisions that any of us might make.

During early student years I seem to have been somewhat on my guard as to the attractions of the opposite sex. Maybe having three sisters, to whom I was very attached, had something to do with it, and during and after university years I was blessed with a multitude of friendships of all ages and both sexes. Apparently I was not quite like the young curate who was a bit too keen on the girls. On being rebuked by his bishop, he replied that he thought that there was safety in numbers. 'More safety in exodus,' growled the bishop.

Our Christian Students Fellowship at university had a fairly equal membership of men and women, and on our committee, at our general meetings, beach missions and social occasions, we mixed cheerfully together but with almost no pairing off at that stage. I sometimes thought, 'I wonder . . . she *is* rather nice,' but nothing came of it.

60

On the morning of Wednesday, April 13th, 1932, quite suddenly and unexpectedly, the answer came. I was having my usual early morning quiet time in Blenheim before catching the morning service car to Christchurch when I felt a clear conviction and assurance that my prayers were answered.

The clarity with which the enlightment came was almost like a shock and was quite unexpected. It was certainly not an audible voice from heaven, but it was something like it. Time was needed to get accustomed to the idea and to think and pray about the implications; in fact a couple of months would elapse before a personal meeting could take place.

At this point I must go back to my arrival in Dunedin in 1931, where I made my home with the Cree Brown family. The Scottish atmosphere of this home and its setting in the more general Scottish atmosphere of Dunedin and its university was most congenial. There was porridge for breakfast and stories about 'Wee McGregor' and his 'Aunt Purdie'; all good nourishment for a fellow Scot. As I mentioned earlier, the Cree Browns had four children, and staying with them during university studies was their niece Florence Marion Thomson. It was the thought of her which had come so vividly that April morning. I noted the initials 'F.M.T.' in my diary opposite the 'F' and 'M' private code.

Marion had become one of the foundation members of the little group of evangelical students. Her parents and her four sisters and brother lived in Hawera in the North Island where her father was in medical practice. We had been together at the two students' houseparties at Karitane near Dunedin, but no idea of marriage had entered either my head or my heart at that stage.

It was a different story when we had another student's houseparty, this time at a beautiful seaside group of holiday cottages at Purakanui, twelve miles from Dunedin. In between meetings we went botanising and discovered a common interest in our love of nature. I found a good excuse to help her to scrape the porridge pots at the kitchen door, and I must have kept my secret very well because she didn't guess.

By this time I knew her well enough to know that behind her quiet and unassuming manner was a young woman of ability, unselfishness, good judgment and mental balance. She loved her work at the university and did well in her classes, botany being her main subject. Of slender build she was quick and alert in her movements and was never happier than when out botanising with friends on the hills around Dunedin, or spending an evening playing classical music at the piano, or with her knitting and a book by the fire on a winter evening. Above all she was a fully committed Christian.

On the morning of Sunday, June 19th, 1932, I woke at four a.m. and said to myself 'This is it.' It was good to have a few hours for quiet and prayer. The SU reading for the day began with the words, 'Wherefore when we could no longer forbear . . .' from 1 Thessalonians 3:1, and included the words of verses 11 and 12; 'Now God himself and our Father, and our Lord Jesus Christ, direct our way unto you. And the Lord make you to increase and abound in love one toward another and toward all men . . .'

I am no believer in getting guidance from opening the Bible at random and suddenly spotting a guidance verse, but there are rare and very special occasions when a verse of Scripture, occurring in the regular course of one's reading, suddenly fits like a key to a lock. Of far greater importance is an understanding of the broad principles of scriptural teaching. But when that is not neglected, and when there has been a background of regular and faithful prayer, the occasional gem occurring at the right time and the right place, cannot be denied its relevance, its confirmation and its comfort.

I took 'Uncle Cree' and later 'Aunt Kathleen' into my confidence. We went together to the evening service at the cathedral, not their usual place of worship. I was somewhat startled as the Dean announced the opening hymn:

> Thy way, not mine, O Lord
> However dark it be;
> Lead me by Thine own hand,
> Choose Thou the path for me.

Although this was a little foreboding I compared the words to the marriage service which underline the principle of 'for better, for worse'. The succeeding verses were, however, more encouraging:

> I dare not choose my lot;
> I would not if I might;
> Choose Thou for me, my God
> So shall I walk aright.
>
> Not mine, not mine the choice,
> In things or great or small:
> Be Thou my Guide, my Strength,
> My Wisdom and my All.
>
> Horatius Bonar

The net was closing round me. I couldn't possibly escape now, and what's more I didn't want to.

Marion had not been with us in the cathedral; she had been reading to her grandfather, but we met after church. It was raining and we shared an umbrella which was a help at this critical juncture. To my relief Marion accepted my proposal and later when the rain had cleared, we walked home arm in arm in the moonlight.

As if that wasn't enough by way of reassurance, Marion's reading that evening from *Daily Light* included the words of Ephesians 1:4, 'He hath chosen us in him before the foundation of the world, that we should be holy and without blame before him in love.' To this day she wears engraved on the inside of her wedding ring another 'private code'—Eph. 1:4.

Three days later I set off by train for Invercargill. As the train gathered speed and as Dunedin fell behind, a feeling akin to consternation came over me. What *had* I done? Was it going to be all right? No doubt some sort of reaction was not altogether abnormal, but I was rather surprised and embarrassed at this mixture of emotions. However, a quiet review of the whole chain of events calmed my fears. The commitment having been made, the doubt could not be countenanced for a moment. From now on it was 'for better, for worse', and for us it turned out to be 'for better'.

After our engagement I found myself thinking about getting married and the possibility of settling down in some quiet corner, but Marion would have none of it. 'We've got some special work ahead of us of some kind, and we have to find out what it is.' Later when we were married she said, 'You've got your work to do, go ahead and do it, and I'll back you up'; and that is exactly what she has done ever since. As the years passed the warmth of her affectionate nature developed and it became most literally true that we 'lived happily ever after'.

Sir Richard Steele, the eighteenth-century English essayist gives me the words I want: 'To behold her is an immediate check to loose behaviour; to love her is a liberal education'.

But over the years Marion and I have known some who have prayed and sought guidance every bit as carefully and earnestly, and have started out as hopefully as we did, and yet their marriage has been less, or even far less than ideal. There has been suffering, mental and emotional; yet the pain has been borne with courage. No easy release from binding promises has been sought. Children have been cared for and not irresponsibly cast off. Both John Wesley and F. B. Meyer had unhappy marriages; yet both brought blessing and happiness to multitudes.

From then on, and often throughout succeeding years, I have recalled two acts of commitment, two leaps of faith, as significant above all others. The first was as a boy of seventeen at the Scripture Union camp in a Scottish glen, when I made a whole-hearted commitment to the leadership of Christ; the other was when I made an equally whole-hearted commitment to a lifetime partnership with my wife, Marion. Both of these commitments have brought enrichment and fulfilment far beyond my best hopes and dreams. They were no mere chance!

Our official engagement was announced on Marion's twenty-first birthday, July 26th, 1932, and a few days later I paid my respects to Dr. and Mrs. Thomson in Hawera. I found myself welcomed into yet another Christian family, with strong Scottish roots. Some of their forbears had emigrated to New Zealand from Ayrshire in Scotland in 1842.

So the prayer about 'M' was answered. We now faced the question of 'F' our future field of service, but with this difference, we faced it together.

In 1932 we were still suffering from the worldwide economic

depression. Back in England, unemployment stood at 2.8 million, and in Russia, starvation had reached disastrous proportions. Even in the normally peaceful country of New Zealand there was some rioting and looting in some of the main cities. Someone explained New Zealand's problem with devastating simplicity — 'We are a country flowing with milk but not with money'.

Partly for this reason, and partly because the infant organisation of the Crusader Movement had not yet developed a sufficiently strong structure I accepted a cut in salary from £5 to £3 a week, but even then my salary was, at one time, two months in arrears.

Through my contact with Dr. Gordon Anderson I got a temporary job in Wellington Hospital. The hospital welcomed my application, as they were short-staffed at the time. I was there from 1st September to 8th December 1932. By the end of that period the financial position had improved somewhat and I was able to resume full-time Christian work again.

In some respects I enjoyed returning to medical work, but the hospital seemed to be going through a bad patch. The overall administration was weak, morale was poor and the medical staff at that time did not seem to have high moral standards, although most were professionally ambitious. On one occasion I seemed to be the only medical officer who was not the worse for drink and preoccupied with visiting girl friends who had been brought in. Bottles and windows were smashed and a clock, a piano and billiard cues were broken and damaged. But most days it was a case of work from nine a.m. until ten thirty p.m. or later, a soul-destroying routine. Competition within the profession seemed to be acute and the staff had to devote themselves to the job with complete concentration. Perhaps that is why, when they did break loose, they did it with a vengeance.

The whole situation seemed a poor alternative to the great work in which I had been engaged. I wrote to my parents: 'To tell you the truth, my heart is not in my medical work. My heart *is* in the winning of souls to Christ and in helping those who are young in the faith to a deeper and fuller spiritual life.'

In spite of the busy hospital programme I managed to fit in preaching most Sundays and helped to organise arrangements for a beach mission at Titahi Bay, some miles to the north of Wellington. I was also involved at this time in the planning of four CSSMs and the Ponui Island camp. Dealing with a considerable correspondence filled in any odd moments.

A letter which gave me food for thought came in November from Mr. Hubbard, the Secretary of the CSSM in London. In this, he strongly encouraged me to accept an appointment on the staff of the CSSM, assuring me that the London Council would most warmly welcome this. Hitherto our New Zealand organisation had been independent and without official links with the CSSM and Scripture Union worldwide. Now I was being offered official recognition by the London Council.

Ever since my days, many years earlier, as a student leader at Elie CSSM in Scotland, Mr. Hubbard had been a source of encouragement and wisdom. To me he was the wise man of Wigmore Street and I respected his counsel and the invitation he had conveyed to me. I knew that he had done his best to find a suitable successor for our work in New Zealand, but without success, and I knew that I dare not leave these flourishing new developments without adequate leadership. In view of all this, Mr. Hubbard's encouragement and invitation weighed all the more heavily. I was truly at the crossroads.

The highlight of my time in hospital was Marion's arrival from Dunedin after she had finished her exams for the B.Sc. degree. It was a warm summer morning when I left the hospital and went with her to catch the ten o'clock New Plymouth express for her home in Hawera. During the long train journey we had plenty of time to discuss our future plans, which were conflicting and confusing. Marion's parents wanted her to have a year's experience of housekeeping, while she would have liked to do a year's study and training at the Bible Training Institute in Auckland.

She had been interested in missionary work for some time. I shared with her my sense of call to service with the CIM, while at the same time keeping in mind Bishop Mowll's advice which he had given me on another memorable train journey. I told her that New Zealand seemed such a rich and blessed land in contrast to China's need and that despite everything I could not forget my missionary 'call' during my student and early post-graduate years.

As we went on discussing these possibilities, I found myself reviewing the time I had spent in New Zealand since the *Northumberland* docked at Auckland in December 1930. For the most part this had been a time full of joy and apparent effectiveness. I had been at full stretch month after month. Our 'parish' covered the whole of New Zealand. Five camps for boys had been held and beach missions had been organised at Takapuna and Brown's Bay. Seldom a week went by without someone coming to a saving faith in Christ; or being counselled; or a message being given in a school assembly; or to a smaller group. There were also church services and personal talks and discussions, often late into the night. As we talked the importance of all this was brought home to us with even greater conviction.

When one sees so many senior schoolboys and girls and students being converted month after month, what *can* one do but go ahead? This is the only thing in the world worth living for, and compared with the healing of people's bodies (which others can do quite well) or making money, there's no comparison at all. The student and school-age groups are of paramount importance for the future of the church and the world. So I thought then and still do now.

It seemed that my work at this stage was mainly evangelistic. If this pattern was to be continued it would mean constant travel away from home, not exactly a suitable job for a married man. We went over the pros and cons as the train sped on its way. Marion was unmoved. If this was God's call she was prepared to back me up, if necessary, at considerable cost to our home life. If the call to China was God's will, she was prepared for that also. Her straightforward thinking and practical common sense were invaluable to me then, as they are now. I recalled her words at the time of our engagement, 'God has some work for us to do and we must find out what it is and do it.'

At the end of the train journey we had still not finally

67

decided, but Marion had certainly helped me to clarify my thinking and to show me that she was with me all the way.

So our New Plymouth Express, hauled by its old steam engine with its cow-catcher in front, steamed eventually into Hawera, where we were met by Dr. Thomson and some of Marion's family.

On one occasion Marion, her family and I set out for a picnic on the slopes of Mount Egmont. We two went off for a walk on our own and made our way along the scrubline, Marion botanising as we went. The mountain was wonderful. There, stretching far below and away into the distance were the farms and towns of Taranaki spread before us like a living map. The conical snow-capped peak, to our disappointment, was covered with mist. Again we talked about our future which seemed so uncertain and perplexing, and then prayed together. Turning to look upwards, we saw that the clouds had parted and the cone-shaped, snow-clad summit was glittering in the afternoon sun, as the clouds which had wrapped it earlier in the day gradually thinned and then drifted gently off like delicate gossamer gleaming in the sun. Then, all too soon the mists drew on again and the peak was hidden.

This little incident came as a symbol that the mists surrounding our future would clear away too, but that in the meantime we must be content with only a glimpse of what lay ahead. So we decided to take a positive step by applying to the China Inland Mission, leaving the decision in God's hands.

With great reluctance I returned to Auckland on December 20th and was soon involved in discussions with Mr. Conway, Home Director of the CIM and other friends. This led to a formal application to the CIM. While we were both quite fit the medical report indicated that we could both be at risk from tuberculosis if we worked in large Chinese cities. Che foo, on the other hand, was a healthy place.

During the next few weeks negotiations were in abeyance as most people were on holiday. I was leading the CSSM at Takapuna followed by the boys' camp at Ponui Island, with a few days at Brown's Bay.

One evening while walking in the dark, I saw a single star reflected in a little pool of water and was reminded that I had read somewhere, 'Faith is the receptacle for omnipotence.'

The CIM council met on Sunday afternoon, January 29th, 1933, and with the exception of Mr. Conway, unanimously decided to decline our offer of service, pending consultation with Mr. C. N. Lack, the Australasian home director, who would shortly be coming to New Zealand.

This decision came as quite a surprise, as Mr. Conway had indicated that it would be otherwise. As far as we could gather their decision was based partly on medical grounds, and partly on the importance some members of the CIM council attached to the work we were already doing in New Zealand. Mr. Lack was due in New Zealand in March. The final decision lay with him, so we had to mark time.

On the morning following the CIM council meeting I was rereading Genesis, still under the stimulating and somewhat spiritualising interpretation of W. A. Orange. That morning at my bedside at Dr. Pettit's home, I came to Genesis 26, verses 2–4: 'And the Lord appeared unto Isaac and said "Go not down into Egypt; dwell in the land which I shall tell thee of: sojourn in this land, and I will be with thee, and will bless thee, for unto thee and thy seed, I will give all these countries, and I will perform the oath which I sware unto Abraham thy father; . . . and in thy seed shall all the nations of the earth be blessed." '

To me as I prayed and pondered the meaning became clearer. Transposed into my circumstances at the moment, the message was, 'Go not to China; sojourn in New Zealand and I will bless thee . . . and in thy spiritual seed shall all (or at least some) of the nations be blessed.'

There was in my mind an emphasis on 'sojourn', a temporary residence only, and the dream and hope was that many of the young New Zealanders I had met would, in time, become seed to be planted in far more 'mission fields' than the one which had been closed to us.

Then on February 15th a telegram arrived offering me a ship's surgeoncy on the *Port Napier* sailing from Wellington to England on March 11th. This was an astonishing development as I had not applied for a job with the Port Line. My immediate reaction was to turn it down, but once again, surprisingly, Dr. Pettit said, 'Why not take it?' His reaction took me unawares, as he had always been so keen to keep me in New Zealand.

However, as I thought it over, it seemed to be the right thing to do. It would enable me to confer with my father and also with Mr. Hubbard as to whether to return to medical work, or to join the staff of the CSSM and Scripture Union for service in New Zealand. Moreover it seemed wise to take the opportunity of a free passage when it came. If I had turned it down it might have been a long time before a similar opportunity occurred.

I asked my fiancée if she could get married at three weeks' notice, and the answer was yes! So I sent a telegram of acceptance to the shipping company and began preparations for leaving New Zealand. Mr. Lack, on his arrival, accepted our decision as being the right one and so in this strange way the door to China was once again closed.

Marion and I were married in St. John's Presbyterian Church, Hawera, on March 8th, 1933, and we set off for the first two days of our honeymoon to Mount Egmont in her father's old model T. Ford. Marion drove the car. We narrowly avoided a serious accident on a single track mountain road, but her skilful driving saved the day.

On March 14th we sailed from Wellington on the *Port Napier* via Cape Horn. On arrival in England we were the guests of Mr. and Mrs. Hubbard in their pleasant home in Great Missenden. The valley below was rich with spring flowers and the bluebell woods were at their best. We had some lovely talks with Mr. Hubbard, interrupted by his careful reading of the football results on Saturday night.

My first task on reaching my home in Kilmacolm was to discuss the future with my father. We talked late into the night at times with considerable emotion. As his only son it had meant much to him that I had set out on a medical career. He had great hopes for my future, and it had been an acute disappointment to him when I turned aside from it. During student days he had supported me financially, so I put it to him that I was prepared to return to medical practice for some years in order to earn the money to repay him for what he had spent on my education. Indeed, a major reason for our visit was to discuss this possibility. To my astonishment, my father told me that only a few days earlier the postman had delivered a letter to my stepmother from a firm

70

of lawyers, advising her that she had inherited a considerable legacy.

It appears that some family money should have gone to my maternal grandmother, but she declined to receive it because it had been earned from the profits of a whisky distillery owned by her family. Having lived for much of her life in Glasgow, she had seen some of the terrible effects of alcoholism among the poor and had adopted strong temperance principles. However the money remained in the family and eventually reverted to us.

This was the story my father told me that night. He thanked me for the offer to refund my university expenses but said that there was now no need for it.

The lawyer's letter had arrived only a few days before we did. As on several occasions in the past, timing had been crucial. Had the money come a few months later, my father might have accepted my offer and I would have been committed to medicine with its demands and limitations for some years to come. As it was, I was able to pursue my calling to full time service on the staff of the Children's Special Service Mission and the Scripture Union. It was no mere chance!

On June 2nd, 1933, I was officially appointed by the London council of the CSSM as their staff worker for New Zealand. Hitherto I had served under the council of the New Zealand Crusader Movement. This I would continue to do, but with the added status of membership of the worldwide movement.

Before we left England, Mr. Hubbard said to me: 'The council of the CSSM will be glad if, in your work in New Zealand, you are a good children's evangelist and a successful leader of the work, but what they are looking for in you above all else is that you should be a man of God.'

Thus the years of uncertainty came to an end. The way to China had not opened, my father had released me from all financial obligations, and I could now see clearly that my life's work was to be in the service of the society which I loved and which had nursed me in my faith.

During these years some principles of guidance emerged. The two great principles of divine sovereignty and human responsibility were both operative. First, there was the consciousness, dim and fading at times, almost overwhelmingly strong at others, of a divine over-ruling Providence, an unseen guiding hand, when things seemed to be taken out of my hands. On other occasions the responsibility for certain decisions was clearly up to me.

Wise decisions are a compound of experience, courage, intuitiveness, imagination, knowledge of the facts, willingness to take risks and awareness of the possibility of failure. Sometimes our decisions will be mistaken and wrong. What should we do then? The important thing is to be sufficiently honest to admit frankly that a mistake *has* been made and not to bluff it out and go ahead in pride, but to be willing to go back and start again, even if it involves some embarrassment. The man who never made a mistake never made anything, and there are times when we have to take the plunge in faith and hope, and strike out for the other side of the river.

When the prayer life is active and steadfastly maintained day by day and over the years, this is a great safeguard against foolish and ill-judged decisions. With growth and spiritual maturity, a healthy instinct can be developed, intuitively warning of danger or prompting to go ahead. Similarly, a constant, systematic and well-balanced daily reading of Scripture and meditation helps to shape modes of thought and implants certain broad principles of right and wrong. Scripture is largely biographical and the constant study of the triumphs and disasters of the men and women represented is immensely instructive.

The prompting or restraining influence of the Holy Spirit upon our spirit must never be divorced from the Word of God in Scripture. If we look to the Holy Spirit alone without the Word we can lay ourselves open to great delusions.

It is helpful to remember that some of God's greatest saints and responsible leaders have not always been clear what to do, and because actions and decisions could no longer be delayed, they have had to move forward in the dark, hardly knowing whether the Lord was really with them or not. Both Hudson Taylor and D. E. Hoste had such experiences in their leadership of the China Inland Mission.

The more I became involved in increasing responsibilities in Christian service, the less I found myself thinking of guidance and the more of duty. If someone whom I esteemed, or some responsible council or committee asked me to do a job, it could not be turned down lightly.

Surely our greatest happiness comes to us when we are working for some great cause in which we enthusiastically believe, and when we can say from the heart: 'I delight to do thy will, O my God; thy law is within my heart.'

6   GROWTH AND JUBILEE

On returning to New Zealand we made our home in Wellington. It was the obvious location as a centre from which to cover the schools of the dominion with regular annual visits. Auckland was well supplied with flourishing churches and evangelical agencies, but Wellington was somewhat barren from a Christian point of view and therefore something of a mission field in itself.

There was a feeling in some quarters that Aucklanders were too insular in terms of the country as a whole, just as later we in London were sometimes thought to be too 'London-minded'. Being already firmly established in Auckland the council continued to be located there. This necessitated my sitting up all night on a wearisome train journey to attend the council meetings three or four times a year.

We found a small house to rent high up on Mount Victoria with a magnificent view but with an approach of 152 steps. This presented no problems when we started off but when the babies arrived, Graham in 1934 and Margaret in 1935, we moved to a bungalow right down on the level within easy access of transport and the shops and very easy for our many visitors to find.

We had not been in Wellington long before I met Clif Reed. He had recently arrived from Dunedin, where his uncle, A. H. Reed, had a flourishing Sunday school supplies business. Clif had been given the task of opening a branch in Wellington. He and I quickly became friends, and an arrangement was made whereby he agreed to import CSSM and other evangelical publications from England and make them available in New Zealand.

At 182 Wakefield Street on the ground floor of Wakefield Chambers, there was a small barber's shop. When this became vacant we installed Dora Palmer (now Mrs. Ron Taylor) as bookshop manager, while upstairs on the fifth floor we opened a small office for the CSSM and Crusader Movement, with Mary Milner in charge.

The years 1934 and 1935 were comparatively uneventful. The routine visiting of schools from one end of the country to another occupied Margaret McGregor and myself, together with meetings, missions, rallies and church services. Fifteen camps were held in 1935 and a special 'Life with a capital L' campaign was held in Christchurch.

One of our main aims during this period was to draw together three organisations which had grown up separately in New Zealand, but which were so similar both in their historical roots and in their aims and ideals that unification seemed the obvious course.

The visit of Howard Guinness in 1930 sponsored by the infant IVF in London, and the formation of Crusader Unions in the schools, was quite unconnected with older existing Scripture Union foundations which had been operating since 1880. There was much to be said for drawing the two together but understandably some were reluctant to co-operate. They preferred to deal directly with Mr. Hubbard, who had faithfully corresponded with them for many years. Gradually, however, the new regime was recognised and accepted. Thus new developments, schools, camps and beach missions, were grafted on to these historic Scripture Union roots.

The New Zealand council of the Crusader Movement, anxious to maintain their independence, were at first reluctant to link up with the CSSM in London of which they knew little; but here again goodwill was gradually established and international links began to grow. We could now see the general strategy which was emerging and could look back on the wonderful way God had guided us.

At a public meeting in Auckland in October 1935, five years after Howard Guinness' visit, a general strategic plan was explained. It was pointed out that in a small country of a million and a quarter people, there were 203 secondary schools and some 35,400 pupils. In Europe at that time Germany was training the Hitler Youth to fanatical enthusiasm, and Italy, too, was training her youth in nationalist movements. Indeed, Mussolini's orders to his youth printed on their membership cards were: 'I undertake to obey the orders of the Duce without question and to serve the Fascist revolution if necessary with my blood.'

Our task in New Zealand was to inspire her youth with an enthusiastic and intelligent loyalty to Christ. It has been reckoned that seventy per cent of all Christians are converted before they reach nineteen years. If that is so, then wisely conducted youth movements are evangelistically of great importance.

One could not but admire the far-sightedness of the Roman Catholic leadership in their plans for the religious education of their children. At real self-sacrifice they raised large sums of money to build and staff their schools, thus providing for their future leadership at lay and clerical level. Because of the government policy of secular education in the schools, the New Zealand Protestant churches had organised a programme of Bible teaching known as 'Bible in schools', but this related only to primary schools. Now, with open doors in nearly all the state secondary schools, well-educated and thoughtful boys and girls were being won for Christ and gaining valuable experience in witnessing in a secular environment, and this was being done with a comparatively small financial outlay. There were no expensive projects in building or property. The state provided the excellent buildings, extensive playing fields and the skilled tuition; our task was to fan into flame the smouldering potential. Right from the beginning, there was a strong emphasis on the importance of conservative, strongly ethical evangelism. Care was taken to avoid short-cuts and emotionalism for its own sake. The evangelistic reaping was mostly done in the camps rather than in the schools.

The nationwide impact which, by the grace of God, we were able to see was very considerable. The Crusader movement came increasingly to hold a strategic position in the religious life of the country. In most of the larger schools there were well-established and recognised groups of boys and girls being encouraged in Christian witness, and we followed the plan of concentrating on the schools and leaving the university students more or less to look after themselves. In the long run, this concentration on the school field resulted in an increasingly strong witness at university level. This resulted in a stream of Christian men and women going into the teaching profession, where in turn many of them did all they could to help the Crusader witness in the schools.

The impact on the churches was cumulative. In the early 1930s there were very few evangelical clergy in the Church of England, apart from the Nelson Diocese. Ten to fifteen years later there were scattered throughout the country a number of evangelical clergy, the first fruits of William Orange's Bible class (known as the 'Orange Pips') and of the Crusaders and IVF. This resulted in a recognised evangelical party in the Anglican Church while other denominations benefited in a similar way. Ex-Crusaders and ex-IVF members were found in leading positions in the government, in business and other spheres of life, and missionary witness in many countries was stimulated. In this the New Zealand Bible Training Institute (now the Bible College of New Zealand) played an important part, and a steady flow of missionaries fanned out across the world.

The Scripture Union as a Bible reading movement has a great tradition of faithful work by honorary SU secretaries and there are still many thousands all over the world. They faithfully run their Scripture Union branches, keep records of membership, send out membership cards and notes, sometimes supplemented by personal letters, pray for their members, and arrange an occasional meeting.

Here is the story of one of them. I first met Mrs. Heath in Christchurch about the time of the 'Life with a capital L' campaign in 1935. She lived in Hanmer, eighty-five miles north of Christchurch, where the hot springs and sharp mountain air attracted visitors.

This shy little lady ran a sweet shop in the village. She was fond of children, many of whom were her regular customers, and she often prayed that she might find some way of speaking to them about the Christian life. Then it occurred to her to use Scripture Union. She got a supply of cards with easy selections of Bible readings, and collected the annual membership fee of two pence. Some of the children had no Bible, and money to buy them was scarce. Her plan was to supply them with junior notes, and the attractive green and gold badge with a golden lamp, but again the shortage of money was the problem.

So Mrs. Heath suggested a sale of work and the children set to, aided by Mrs. Heath and their parents; all sorts of goodies were made and set out for sale, the vicar declared it open, and

77

the money came rolling in. At the end of the day, wonderful to relate, there was enough in hand to pay for all that was needed. This was followed a little later by a ceremony when the badges were publicly presented to the members but on one condition, that the badges would only be worn when the member was faithfully reading the daily 'portion'. If they had stopped reading, or missed a few days, no badge was to be worn. The result was that when Mrs. Heath spotted one of her members without a badge, she made her gentle enquiries and this occasionally resulted in a visit to mother, who might herself become a Scripture Union member, and perhaps start family worship in the home.

Blessings on your memory, dear Mrs. Heath! You were one of many thousands of faithful SU secretaries who have, in quiet and unassuming ways, led many thousands to the feet of Christ.

1936 was a year full of excitement and development with a full programme of speaking engagements, but if at all possible, I always managed to be in Wellington for the first Saturday evening of the month for what we called the Scripture Union rallies in the Congregational church hall. They were, in fact, more in the nature of a large-sized Bible class, with an attendance of about one hundred young adults, the upper age limit of admission being thirty years. This monthly Bible teaching ministry had been my wife's idea, and although she could not attend herself because of the care of the children, she gave the strongest moral and practical support behind the scenes.

The teaching each month consisted of a straightforward lecture, lasting about an hour, on the book we were currently reading in our SU portions including practical application. On some occasions, however, some topical subjects were dealt with such as Temptation, Guidance, Worldliness, Is the Bible True? and, of course, Love and Marriage. Maintaining a fairly high level of teaching involved much hard work, but of all the things that I look back on in the New Zealand days, these monthly teaching opportunities stand out as among the best. I think I can honestly say that I received as much, if not more, than I put in by way of feedback and personal fulfilment.

As soon as the summer beach missions were over, it seemed that the moment had come to consolidate and draw together the small but growing groups of evangelical students which now existed in nearly all the colleges, so it was decided to hold a conference over the Easter holidays.

A small organising committee was set up in Wellington and on Good Friday, April 10th, 1936, thirty-four young men and women assembled. Numbers were small but they represented great potential for the future. The four student presidents representing Auckland, Wellington, Christchurch and Dunedin all made their mark as Christian leaders in later years.

During this first Easter Conference, Dr. Pettit came from Auckland and gave us an interesting historical perspective. He spoke of the first Student Christian Movement in 1896 when John Mott, from America, was one of the speakers. In the years that followed student summer conferences were held with sound Bible teaching, but as time went on, the doctrinal basis of the Movement was widened and became increasingly influenced by liberal theology. Eventually Dr. Pettit and his friend Cree Brown felt that they must withdraw, and Cree Brown became leader of a small Bible class in Dunedin. About the same time (1927) a group of students began to meet in Auckland forming the first Evangelical Union in New Zealand.

We have already seen how William Orange's Bible class had started independently of what was happening in Auckland and Dunedin. All this had prepared the way for Howard Guinness' arrival in October 1930 with news of evangelical student movements in England, Scotland, Canada and Australia, injecting a new spirit of enthusiasm and confidence into these small informal groups. Someone remarked that Guinness, the Irishman, had led the cavalry charge while Laird, the Scotsman, had followed on and built the bridges.

Thus our hurriedly arranged Easter conference was the next step forward in a movement which today far exceeds the hopes and expectations of these early years, for it eventually became part of the International Fellowship of Evangelical Students, a worldwide movement of great significance in the life of the church and the student world, which had played an important part in the promotion of evangelical scholarship, and in education, medicine, law and other fields, and out-standingly in its publications and missionary outreach.

During these years my work had been mainly that of an evangelist and teacher with some organising thrown in. With the growth of the movement and the appointment of younger men and women to do the travelling and the schools visitation, the emphasis began to change to administration, until in later years, rather to my regret, it became my full-time vocation.

1939 was a memorable year. It was the year of the Diamond Jubilee of the Scripture Union and J. H. Hubbard, with his small team of secretaries, had worked indefatigably to make it an outstanding success. Once more I got a job as a ship's surgeon, this time on the *Port Auckland*, and we sailed for London round Cape Horn.

It was a splendid journey with magnificent rolling waves, our ship laboriously climbing up to the crest and then sliding down the other side. Great albatrosses floated over us hundreds of miles from the nearest land, and there were magnificent views of Cape Horn in lovely weather. The ship was covered with a light sprinkling of snow and I thought what fun it would be to tee up and drive a golf ball on to the land. But of course, it was much too far away. There were glimpses of penguins and other sea-going birds, and when we reached the equator we indulged in all sorts of nonsense, eventually berthing at King George V Docks, London, on March 10th.

I reported to Mr. Hubbard at his home in Great Missenden and was mildly ticked off for not arriving a fortnight earlier. He had arranged an impressive series of meetings beginning in Ireland and Scotland.

My travelling companions were R. T. Archibald and Dick Hudson Pope. Roddy Archibald was the beloved leader of the CSSM in India where he spent forty-five years as an evangelist to India's children, while Dick Pope served as a children's evangelist in England for an unbroken half-century. He excelled as a teaching-evangelist, and as with Roddy, hundreds if not thousands of Christian men and women could date their conversion to Christ to their response at one of his missions. The more I got to know these men of God the more I admired them for their integrity of character and personal saintliness. A note in Roddy's old Bible reads: 'Live by your admirations, not your disgusts.' This I had no difficulty in doing in the company of two such men.

On our way from Birmingham to Stafford, Dick Pope and I called on the Owens of Sutton Coldfield. Alfred Owen, later Sir Alfred Owen of Rubery Owen, a big industrial concern, lived with his family in one of the oldest inhabited houses in England. Surrounded by a moat, parts of the house were of the twelfth century. The panes in some of the windows were made of horn before glass came into general use. I noticed an old tapestry which had been worked by a child at school, with the following verse:

Adam alone in Paradise doth grieve
And thought Eden a desert without Eve,
Until God, pitying his lonesome state,
Crowned all his wishes with a lovely mate.
What reason then hath man to slight or doubt her
That could not live in Paradise without her!

It was generally recognised at this time that war might come but people didn't seem to be greatly concerned. The weather was glorious and everything seemed prosperous. Britain under Chamberlain had adopted an appeasement policy towards Hitler, while Churchill repeatedly warned the country of the danger to come. Conscription was introduced. As in 1914, these were golden days with a false atmosphere of peace and safety before the breaking of the storm.

At the end of June 1939, I attended as a delegate from New Zealand the fourth International Conference of Evangelical Students at Cambridge. There were nearly 800 students present from thirty-three countries, including many distinguished speakers from Europe.

The largest contingent of 200 students came in a specially chartered ship from Norway. They were led by Professor O. Hallesby of Oslo. Several years previously I had read his book on prayer and had been much moved and helped by it, especially the last chapter 'The Spirit of Prayer'. Of all the speakers he impressed me most and so did the quality of the young men and women from Norway. Little did I imagine that one day in the distant future Marion and I would be the grandparents of three young Norwegians, for in 1969 our daughter Janet married Bent Reidar Eriksen, a Norwegian

81

pastor, trained in the Free Faculty of Theology where Professor Hallesby had been a leading personality for several decades.

The timing of the conference proved to be of great significance as it was the last such gathering before Europe was plunged into the darkness of war. Although we did not know this at the time, we may be sure that the conference helped to cement evangelical friendship which war could not sever, and it prepared the students and their leaders, especially in Europe, for the great ordeal they were about to face.

On my visits to London from Scotland and later, on several occasions from New Zealand, I always found time for lengthy discussions with Douglas Johnson. This remarkable man, for forty-one years general secretary of the Inter-Varsity Fellowship of Evangelical Unions (now the Universities and Colleges Christian Fellowship), exercised his far-reaching ministry with a minimum of travel. He remained in London and people came to him. He rarely spoke in public, but spent endless time in personal conversations, committees and letter-writing. His self-effacing modesty is proverbial. He was a voracious reader, and although he would probably deny it, a far-sighted strategist.

We two had much in common, for we both came from a similar background in our early youth, were medically trained and yet had spent the greater part of our lives in maintaining the evangelical faith and promoting evangelism through youth and student work, he with the IVF and I with the CSSM and Scripture Union.

In our 1939 discussions Douglas Johnson held forth at great length on the importance of having in one's mind an adequate theological and philosophical frame of reference and an 'overall stategic concept'. Whether approached historically, theoretically or practically, he stressed that the main aim which must never be lost sight of was that our movement should be energetically evangelistic. He maintained that the unifying and overall purpose was to witness to Christ and to seek continually to bring men and women, boys and girls, to a living faith in Him.

His favourite quotation was from a nineteenth-century author of naval strategy, 'When you are trying to accomplish something you should first decide what is the *final objective* you are seeking to attain, and then *never lose sight of it.*' He hammered home this and many similar ideas to generations of students and colleagues, and exemplified it in his own life.

I still treasure a characteristic letter written by Douglas in August 1940, when the Battle of Britain was at its height. He had been working under heavy stress and had suffered from a heart attack and was confined to bed for a time. He wrote as follows:

After flu, I had a strange feeling on the left side and a numbness on the inner side of the left arm. Electrocardiogram and the cardiologist said 'Slight left coronary occlusion' — result bed for twelve weeks and no work for six months. Result for me: have done more reading than ever! Read more things I have longed to do for years, got real intellectual rest on nearly all the points which have baffled our generation! Hence, feel twice as fit to carry on the work!!! Sorry you aren't here to be bombed with us so that we could spend time in shelters planning the next advance. Looking forward to meeting you again on earth if the Lord doesn't return; if not, then in heaven. N.B. I hope there's a library there!

The threat of war was becoming even more ominous, but it was easy to forget it for the moment as I visited the lovely seaside resorts in perfect summer weather on a speaking tour round the Norfolk coast and the South of England.

Each mission was staffed by a team of voluntary workers paying their own expenses and for the most part under capable and experienced leadership. I got the impression that the standards were high and the teams of workers of a very good type. It was interesting, too, to come across the names of famous evangelical families which kept cropping up in one houseparty after another. The training of workers as a team under good leadership, and the experience of gaining the confidence of parents and children and presenting Christ to them, was quite invaluable. From these seaside missions have come, for over a hundred years, a steady stream of gifted Christian leaders, whose influence has been incalculable.

The glorious summer passed quickly and I was glad to get home to Scotland, where I began to realise that the Jubilee Year had not been a bed of roses for my wife. There were moments when, in spite of all the kindness of my parents and sisters with whom she was staying, she felt desperately homesick for New Zealand and her family. It is not always easy to look after two lively children in someone else's home over a long period and Marion had found it trying, although there had been much kindness and happiness as well.

Looking back to certain incidents, I find myself putting a different interpretation on them now. For instance, one of the children was being persistently naughty and disobedient, even after being scolded or spanked. At the time I thought it was a manifestation of original sin or just plain cussedness, but I now think that at the time the child was desperately unhappy, but did not have the language or power of expression or insight to unburden to an understanding adult. What should have happened was that both parents should have given their unhurried time to the children. This my wife certainly did, but I was often too preoccupied. The children needed an easy and relaxed atmosphere with us both so that the trouble could come out into the open and be lovingly dealt with. This is not to deny that some things in our human nature are wrong and sinful in themselves which we have to confess, seek pardon for, fight against and put right. But we need someone who is experienced and tactful to help us in this. Denunciatory preaching and hard unfeeling attitudes are not the answer.

7 THE SPIRITUAL WAR

Then the blow, long-dreaded and expected, fell. Britain and France declared war on Germany on Sunday morning, September 3rd, 1939. Mr. Chamberlain made the announcement in his dry, matter-of-fact way that a 'state of war exists between us'.

Suddenly all our arrangements for meetings and other activities came to an abrupt halt. It was generally believed that hostilities would begin at once and that Britain would be attacked by gas warfare. Children were evacuated from cities to the country and gas masks were brought out. Our travel arrangements to New Zealand were cancelled. We were completely at a loss to know what to do.

My own thoughts turned to medical work, either in the British army or back in New Zealand. Quite unexpectedly, I was offered a medical appointment at the TB sanatorium at Quarrier's Homes, only a few miles from Kilmacolm. These homes for orphan boys and girls were founded by William Quarrier in 1878.

Perhaps rather impulsively I wrote to the army authorities, offering my services but no reply to this letter was ever received. As the months went by the 'phoney war' continued, and much thought and prayer were given to the next move. Finally, we decided to return to New Zealand where we had our home, where my wife had her family and friends, and where our work awaited us.

We were quite sorry to leave the tranquil life and interesting medical work. It was especially hard for my parents to say good-bye, as my sister Martha was about to sail for nursing missionary work in India. Our youngest sister, Nancy, was also about to set out for similar work in Central Africa with the Brethren. Our eldest sister, Mona, was the only one who remained in Britain and she went on to become a well-loved headmistress. Sadly she died of cancer in the summer of 1961.

We spent Christmas on the *Oronsay* in Southampton

harbour, wreathed in a cold, heavy fog. On the following day the fog lifted, the anti-submarine boom was opened and we set off, working up to full speed and at times zig-zagging to elude submarine attack.

We had a number of missionaries on board and two hundred German Jews, who went ashore at Haifa. We arranged meetings for the children, and on one occasion I was telling them the story of Jairus' daughter who was raised to life by Jesus. When we came to the Lord's words, 'Talitha cumi', one little Jewish boy piped up:

'I know what that means.'

'What does it mean?'

Speaking slowly and groping for the words in English, he replied, 'It means . . . it means . . . it is now time to get up.' The very words still used by Jewish mothers when getting their children up in the morning!

Trans-shipping to the *Wanganella* at Sydney, and after a stormy crossing, we reached our home in Wellington on February 13th, 1940. From that day onwards we were caught up in a busy round of activities. It was good to be back home again with the people and the work we loved, and to be back in our own bungalow on the busy street with the quiet garden behind, which would later have the appendage of an air-raid shelter. During the next few war-years our home became a busy centre for hospitality for men in the forces and visitors passing through Wellington.

In common with many Christian friends, I had deep heart-searchings about the rights and wrongs of military service. I was influenced to some extent by the example of my Quaker friends of schooldays. Personally I would have had little difficulty in serving in a strictly medical capacity and was prepared to do so if called upon. But this seemed an easy way out of the difficulty without having to face the issue in principle. One could only try to share with one's friends their heart-searchings as each had to settle the issue for himself.

Margaret McGregor, Colin Becroft and I took on a full programme of meetings covering nearly the whole dominion. Nearly everywhere we had a good reception, not only from the Christian public but in the schools. I was usually away from home on tour for four months spread throughout the year. On one occasion, after a fairly long absence, Graham asked plaintively, 'How long are you going to stay, Daddy?'

The fifth IVF Conference was held in Wellington from May 11th to 17th, 1940. There were about seventy-five students present and we were involved in all the arrangements. It seemed that our decision to return was fully justified, though we often felt selfish at being in favoured New Zealand when our family and friends were involved in the terrible war in Europe.

'Let us work while it is day for the night cometh when no man can work', was constantly sounding in my ears, and became the theme of many of our messages. The 'night' might indeed have come. After the war we saw samples of Japanese bank notes printed for use in New Zealand in the event of a Japanese military occupation.

By the end of July 1940, the work of the Crusader movement, the CSSM and Scripture Union came to the crossroads. In common with every organisation working among youth, we were faced with increasing difficulties on account of the war and it seemed inevitable that the work would suffer. On the other hand, we realised that never was the work more urgent.

Two possibilities lay before us: one marked extinction and the other extension. We stood at the parting of the ways. Surely it would be folly to plan for extension of Christian work under the restrictive conditions of wartime? Where could we possibly find the workers or the increased financial support? But the idea gradually developed that we should plan a wartime forward move, and at the council meeting of September 30th, it was decided to launch a wartime forward move on all fronts.

One result was to appoint a full-time children's evangelist, and several full-time or part-time regional secretaries to foster the work in the schools and to extend the ministry of Scripture Union Bible reading, leadership training courses, and the sale of carefully selected books. To help in this extra office staff were appointed, and co-operation with other evangelical youth movements was increased. We even dared to hope that:

> The time shall come when like a swelling tide
> The Word shall leap the barriers and light
> Shall sweep the land: and faith and love and hope
> Shall win for Christ the strongholds of the night.

87

The financial side of things began to be sorted out quite quickly once we had decided on a course of action. But there was a shortage of manpower as one by one our male colleagues joined the Forces. Ted Lewis served with the New Zealand Expeditionary Force in North Africa. We greatly missed his cheerful company as did many hundreds of boys and young men to whom he had brought outstanding Christian leadership and inspiration. Colin Becroft's overall leadership and administrative ability was also a great loss. For myself I was Grade II medically and with two, and later four children, was not likely to be enlisted for some time. Eventually I was called up for an interview by Brigadier Bowerbank, head of Army Medical Services. When he heard of the nature of my work he told me that he had been a Scripture Union member when a boy in the north of England, and this meant that he understood the motivation relating to our work. He consulted Bishop Holland, then Bishop of Wellington, and maybe others, and in second and third interviews he told me that because of our work among youth, which he regarded as of national importance, I would not be called up. But he made one stringent condition, namely that if for any reason I were to give up my present work, I should immediately report to him for reconsideration of my case.

Many months later I received a letter from him telling me that he had been ill and enclosing a cheque for five pounds with a request that he wished to renew his Scripture Union membership and become a member of my Reveille branch. This was followed by a formal and strongly-supported appeal by the council of the Crusader Movement which resulted in my being classified as a 'clerk in Holy orders'. Thus being set free I dedicated myself all the more to the spiritual warfare and a battle it certainly was, both exciting and exhausting. It was no time to take things easy. At times like these, in the words of Amos, it was a case of 'Woe to them that are at ease in Zion'. Or to quote the words of the Apostle Paul, 'It is because we realise the importance of the spiritual, that we labour and struggle.' (1. Tim. 4:10, J. B. Phillips.)

Both men and women rallied round enthusiastically. When we became short-staffed and could not travel extensively, we determined that our weapons would be in the form of words and ideas. So we built up the office staff, and under Mary Milner's capable leadership we kept our front-line troops of voluntary workers well posted with news, literature and personal correspondence.

A generous supporter provided a car, thus increasing mobility, and I acquired a portable typewriter and a dictaphone with wax cylinders and a carrying case, so that a steady flow of communication could be maintained. Public meetings in the various centres were well attended and 'Crusader' groups flourished in an ever-increasing number of schools. Every school holiday had its camps either under canvas or in beach cottages or school buildings and the number of beach missions was maintained or increased. As part of the war effort six farming camps were organised.

To promote a campaign to encourage Bible reading one of our supporters paid for a huge roadside poster on the main road leading into Wellington with a picture of an open Bible and the following wording, 'The only way out of the dark.'

At this time it was estimated that out of the total New Zealand population one person in fifty-six was a member of the Scripture Union.

Meantime a deadly threat hung over us: in Europe from Germany, in Australia and New Zealand from Japan. Whenever Churchill made a speech we hung on his words. They were words of encouragement and challenge, but they also faced realistically the possibility of impending disaster. We shared the feelings of the little English girl who, in the worst days of the bombing prayed, 'Dear God, please look after yourself, for if anything happens to you, we're sunk.'

Sons and brothers, husbands and fathers, were being killed and wounded in Europe, North Africa and the Pacific. Those of us who were in the thick of the spiritual warfare found ourselves giving time to prayer individually and collectively as we had never done before, and on more than one occasion the Wellington Town Hall was crowded for a Citizens' Intercessory Service. On one such occasion the Governor General, the Prime Minister and members of the cabinet and parliament were on the platform and I had the awesome responsibility of giving the message, which was broadcast throughout the Dominion.

In the midst of all these exciting events our family life continued normally throughout the war-years. The usual routine was to work at home in the morning dictating letters, talking on the telephone at my roll-top desk or preparing a message for a forthcoming meeting. The afternoon was spent at the office with its magnificent view across the harbour. The cylinders were transcribed, letters signed and visitors seen by appointment; then home by tram in time for tea with the family and bedtime stories for the children. Quite often there would be meetings in the evenings and sometimes men from the armed forces would drop in for an evening meal.

Two more important events of the war-years were the arrival of two more of our children, Janet and Elizabeth. I was leading a beach mission just prior to Janet's birth and prayed earnestly that I would be back with Marion in time for the birth of the baby. I made it with half a day to spare!

No account of the Laird family during the years of the war would be complete without a reference to one of our most formative experiences. A friend came to share our home and stayed for three years, going out to work daily and helping my wife with the household jobs. She came from a remote country area where her mother had died some years earlier, while her father appeared to be still suffering from the effects of the First World War.

All went well in the early months of her stay with us, but when our third child was born she experienced times of depression and difficulty. Inevitably there were emotional tensions and the next three years of living together in our small bungalow imposed considerable strain on us all. The monster depression was hard to bear at times, and we were at a loss to know how to cope with it.

As the years passed various things happened to raise the horizon by slow degrees. My wife encouraged our friend to take classes at the university and to work towards a B.A. degree. While doing a full-time job in an office she worked at her studies, eventually graduating and then qualifying as a teacher with considerable professional success. There were times when faith grew dim. Due to a lack of a strong family background, loneliness surfaced again and again, but eventually the day came when she married and had a family of her own. As a busy wife and mother and an active Christian worker, the loneliness and depression became a thing of the past.

Both my wife and I, who had warm and stable family backgrounds, found it a deep and searching lesson to share our lives with one who had endured the severe emotional stresses arising from a traumatic childhood. We learned more about human nature than we could have learned in any other way. We are all grateful for such a happy outcome, but we realise, too, that our immaturity and inexperience must have contributed to the suffering in which we shared.

Looking back, we have the assurance that it was part of God's overruling for all our lives. It is out of trials and difficulties, lived through and worked through together, that maturity develops, and this proved to be so in our experience.

During our years in Wellington we had many happy associations with the Salvation Army. Our two elder children, Graham and Margaret, attended their Sunday school near to our home and our two youngest, Janet and Elizabeth, were born in a Wellington Salvation Army Maternity Home.

I was once asked to speak at a big youth rally at the Salvation Army Citadel. Suddenly in the prayer room before the meeting began, the door opened and the officer's wife in army uniform produced a handkerchief, and polished the top of her husband's bald head. I must have looked astonished because I was hastily informed that this operation was necessary because their teenage daughter, after a liberal application of lipstick, had kissed her father a fond farewell on the top of his bald head. As this could have proved embarrassing for such a respectable citizen on bowing his head in prayer on a public platform his wife saved the situation and all was well.

Early in 1944 a pressing invitation came from a group of evangelical leaders in Australia, including Canon R. B. Robinson, chairman of the CSSM and Scripture Union in Sydney, Archbishop Mowll, the Rev. Marcus Loane and Dr. Paul White to spend some months helping to build up CSSM, Crusaders and ISCF.

They were particularly concerned because, under wartime conditions, the Australian authorities had planned to launch a youth movement, supported by government funds. This movement would encourage weekends in the country, with character training and short three-minute services on Sundays. They felt that such a secular youth movement had great potential danger, and that the only satisfactory way of countering it would be to build up strong and effective Christian youth movements. Unfortunately the evangelical youth movements were very divided and, to some extent, out of touch with each other. It was agreed that a united front would be a great advantage, and it was thought that I might be able to help in this direction. Accordingly, with the full support of the New Zealand council, I set off on April 14th, 1944, for a three-month visit to Australia.

Some of the problems in Australia dated back to the days of Edmund Clark, who had gone to Australia in 1913 under CSSM auspices, with the reluctant permission of the London council. Mr. Hubbard described him as 'a genius with all the faults of a genius'. He was a brilliant children's evangelist, with a quixotic skill in understanding and helping boys and young men, although in a very unorganised way, and some of those who were influenced by him in their early days became outstanding leaders

Both in Sydney, the largest centre, and in Melbourne and Brisbane, there were vigorous independent evangelical youth movements which had sprung up and been led, for the most part, by able, strong-minded, individualistic leaders who carried on their good work with little reference to each other. These three largest cities were widely separated geographically and this meant that things developed independently to some extent in each state, though efforts were made, with limited success, to keep inter-state communications alive between kindred organisations.

Above all, however, there was the challenge of the war, and hopes for the future when it ended. All these factors had the effect of stimulating thinking as to future developments and the need for greater effectiveness. It seemed, therefore, that my visit was well-timed, as there were stirrings of hope and expectations for better things. At our first meeting in Sydney there were no less than forty representatives of six or seven evangelical youth movements. Several who were present said that it was a unique experience to see the various personalities brought together in this way. These organisations included the CSSM and Scripture Union, Boys' Crusaders, Girls' Crusaders, Boys' Inter-School Christian Fellowship, Girls' Inter-School Christian Fellowship, and the Inter-Varsity Fellowship of Evangelical Unions.

When I met the council of the CSSM for the first time, Archbishop Mowll was in the chair. His links with the CSSM went back to his student days in England. Throughout my visit to Australia, he gave me the utmost encouragement by chairing important meetings, both publicly and in committee, together with a number of private conversations.

The task to which I had been called proved to be interesting but difficult and time-consuming. I had the invaluable help of my friend Alex Brown as we worked, prayed and travelled together. He had been on the staff since 1925 and knew most of the people involved, thus making up for my lack of local knowledge.

It soon became obvious that the need was to find men with the all-round leadership and administrative gifts of general secretaryship, most urgently in New South Wales, but also in Melbourne and Queensland. While Alex Brown and Vincent Craven, both on the staff of the CSSM, were gifted specialists in their own important fields of service, it still seemed necessary to find someone to co-ordinate and administer the work as a whole; to represent it to the public, to build up the finances and, above all, to give a spiritual lead.

It was felt that Vincent Craven had been doing two jobs, his work with boys and his secretarial duties, and that the time had come for him to concentrate on the former and hand over the latter to someone else. During my time in Australia he was on active service with the Y.M.C.A., but he knew that this proposal had been discussed and had expressed his approval of it.

In the course of these negotiations, various anomalies came to light and policy decisions were discussed. Financial support from the Christian public and the payment of adequate remuneration to the staff members were important issues. There were, for instance, differences of opinion as to how funds should be sought. Some pressed for a policy like that of the China Inland Mission, where no appeals were permitted, while others felt that it was legitimate to make the financial needs known and to appeal for help. Lack of unity on this policy resulted in something of a stalemate, with the result that funds were scanty and staff members inadequately provided for.

One thing which became very obvious was that a committee without a full-time executive officer to carry out its decisions and to guide and stimulate it was largely ineffective. Committees can talk and make decisions, but they cannot, in their corporate capacity give a lead, or do evangelism, or exercise pastoral care. What they can do is to appoint someone to do these things and then give him their encouragement, moral support and general guidance. Their main responsibility is to search for the right man or woman. In doing so, they should look for a man of God, of personal integrity, administrative ability and an overall statesmanlike view, together with skill and tact in handling difficult situations and individuals. Such men are very hard to find, especially in wartime when so many were in the armed forces.

In Sydney a small selection committee was eventually set up under the chairmanship of Canon R. B. Robinson. It included the Rev. Marcus Loane, now Archbishop of Sydney and Anglican Primate of Australia, the Rev. Basil Williams, IVF travelling secretary, and Mr. W. E. Porter, headmaster of a large school and a member of one of the Brethren Assemblies of Sydney, and myself.

We had the greatest difficulty in finding and nominating the right man. Some who were suitable were not free, or not willing to serve, or were serving with the armed forces. It was not until the end of our three months in Australia that a member of the council, a Baptist layman, Mr. R. E. Walker, offered to serve as the honorary secretary of the council and as acting general secretary for an interim period of six months. Ron Walker held an important senior position in the Supreme Court as a prothonotary. He was, therefore, a man of experience, wide knowledge and ability, and it was a great step forward when he undertook this responsibility. He told me that the call to offer to do this job was the most definite thing he had ever had in his life. It came suddenly to him in the middle of a sermon which he was preaching, and it hit him like a sledgehammer so that he was hardly able to finish his sermon. Then he was hit by the same call on another occasion, so that he felt unable to avoid the responsibility of offering his services. I told him that his decision was one of the best things that had happened during our discussions in Australia. He had promised to serve for six months but actually did so for nearly two and a half years. In June 1947, he was succeeded as general secretary by the Rev. Basil Williams.

The key personality to emerge in Melbourne was Alan Kerr. He was the chairman of a co-ordinating committee which began to function in February 1944, two months before my arrival. This was very much needed because both in Melbourne and Sydney there had been many difficulties. The Anglicans were suspicious of the Baptists and vice versa. There was a good deal of snobbishness centering on the differences between the fee-paying 'public' schools and the state high schools. There were family strongholds of privilege and influence. There were chairmen and secretaries of committees who jealously guarded their prerogatives, and there were old sores needing healing and help. But many were wonderful people who gave unsparingly and sacrificially of their talents, time and strength. They just needed good leadership, a well-ordered structure and greater width of vision to bring out the best in them.

In these circumstances, Alan Kerr played a notable leadership role. In this way there began for me an association with him which has lasted to the present day, culminating in his outstanding chairmanship of the international council of the Scripture Union worldwide. At one of our conferences in Melbourne a verse from Jeremiah (45:5) was quoted: 'And seekest thou great things for thyself? Seek them not.' This brief word of Scripture went like an arrow to the heart of the young Alan Kerr. It played a formative part in his life as his business grew and prospered into an Australia-wide organisation. In all the busy years that followed, he kept his sense of proportion and gave lavishly and generously of his time to Christian work, while at the same time developing a successful business.

Our many efforts to promote understanding, co-operation and, in some cases, amalgamation, came to a head at an

95

important conference held at the Grange in the Blue Mountains, New South Wales. Here in this beautiful setting on June 30th, 1944, thirty-three delegates gathered for our final conference. The main objective of our discussions related to the problems and future plans for New South Wales, but Alan Kerr was present from Melbourne and reported fully what had been happening there. The Saturday morning of the weekend was spent in giving brief reports, followed in each case by prayer, and this proved to be quite a mountain-peak experience. In that atmosphere of prayer, sharing and fellowship, we were drawn closer to one another and to our common Lord. We found once again that to pray together helped us to stay together, and we began to learn that while the Gospel makes us free, it does not make us independent.

One result of our many discussions and committee meetings was to encourage the evangelical youth movements in each state to work closely together within the state boundaries, rather than to attempt to achieve Australia-wide federations of each of them. The policy was, on the whole, adopted, and in the years that followed the internal developments in each state grew in strength. Eventually, in 1954, the time was ripe for the emphasis to be changed from internal state development to federalisation at Australia-wide level.

When flying from Adelaide to Melbourne, I noticed the isolated farmhouses each with its individual waterhole. These farms struck me as being symbolic of an isolationist mentality. Speaking at a meeting in Melbourne that night I referred to the danger of a 'waterhole mentality'. The phrase stuck in the minds of at least some, and served as a reminder of the need for an Australia-wide vision, and later, a world vision. This change in outlook was accelerated by the availability of a special fund of over one thousand pounds which had been put at my disposal by a friend in New Zealand. This money was used to pay the air fares from various Australian states to enable attendance at meetings of the federal council of the CSSM and Scripture Union. One of the main objections to the formation of an Australia-wide federal council had been the cost of travel. One state ruled it out as being altogether too extravagant. The use of this specially allocated money overcame these objections in the initial stages, and by the time the special fund had been used up, the value of inter-state council meetings had become accepted, and funds for air travel had become available from other sources. Gradually inter-state air travel became no longer a luxury but a necessity for any Australia-wide organisation.

Looking back over the three months spent in Australia, we were involved in negotiations with thirteen or fourteen different committees, seven residential conferences and over 150 personal contacts.

These activities were not without their frustrations and struggles, but in all the welter of meetings and interviews new life was coming to birth, yet it could not be hurried. I have been told that I tend to over-elaborate and that I am too much of a perfectionist. This may well be true, but in dealing with complex human situations, short cuts and simplistic solutions are not the answer and this proved to be the case in Australia. Alex Brown, myself and many other men and women in positions of leadership learned increasingly what Paul meant when he spoke of 'the care of all the churches'.

One recurrent problem was a tendency to possessiveness on the part of key personnel in reference to their particular organisation. This seemed to be especially so in the case of truly devoted women, who sometimes exceeded their male counterparts in their devotion to their particular cause and in their reluctance to merge into a wider grouping. It was no easy task to persuade people to take a wider view and to think in terms of what was best for the Kingdom of God rather than their own particular patch. We found that people had to be slowly and patiently educated to lift up their eyes and see the further horizons. This calls for the kind of leadership which D. E. Hoste describes in one of his letters (see D. E. Hoste, China Inland Mission, page 155):

What is the essential difference between spurious and true Christian leadership? When a man, in virtue of an official position in the church, demands obedience of another, irrespective of the latter's reason and conscience, this is the spirit of tyranny.

When, on the other hand, by the exercise of tact and sympathy, by prayer, spiritual power and sound wisdom, one Christian worker is able to influence and enlighten another, so that the latter, through the medium of his own reason and conscience, is led to alter one course and adopt another, this is true spiritual leadership.

It was this quality of leadership which gradually emerged among us during these interesting months, and it was this quality that we had been seeking.

On Saturday, July 8th, Archbishop and Mrs. Mowll invited fifty of us to morning tea at Bishopscourt. This was one of the many kindnesses shown me by the Archbishop and Mrs. Mowll, including being their house guest at Bishopscourt. I little dreamed that the day would come when Marion and I would be the grandparents of four young Mowlls. This came about through the marriage of our daughter Margaret in 1958 to the Archbishop's nephew, Christopher Martyn Mowll. The friendships made during these months in Australia had a real quality of warmth and brotherliness which in some cases have lasted to this day.

The return crossing was made by flying boat to New Zealand on July 20th. It was wonderful to be home again, but I found that the long separation of three months had been quite a trial for my wife. Before leaving for Australia, I had made arrangements for a young girl to keep my wife company, hoping that this would be a helpful plan. Unfortunately, it turned out to be the reverse. My wife had to cope, not only with our three children and a baby, but also with a difficult teenager. Marion and I agreed that to be away from home for as long as three months at a stretch while the children were young was to be avoided as far as possible in the future. She had promised to back me in all my work and she had done so magnificently, but I felt that I must be more careful not to presume on this and to expect too much from her.

During the war-years I had been corresponding with the London office with a view to my joining the secretarial staff there and I only agreed to accept with some reluctance. The New Zealand council were then left with the task of finding my successor. They did not find this easy, but for my part I soon became convinced that Colin Becroft was the man. As one council member, a canny Aberdonian by birth, lay awake one night, his thoughts turned to the account in 1 Samuel 16, of the anointing of the youthful David by Samuel, and the words, 'Arise, anoint him; for this is he,' came to him. From then on he became a firm friend and supporter of Colin Becroft who succeeded me in the leadership of the New Zealand movement on July 20th, 1945.

Colin had been associated with the movement since his schooldays at Auckland Grammar School. In reply to Atholl Donnell's question, 'Are you a Christian?' he had replied indignantly, 'Well, I'm not a heathen!' In 1932, after some hesitation, he became a member of Crusaders in his school and made a definite commitment to Christ at a Ponui Island camp soon afterwards. Colin was a vital, purposeful character, very able and persistent in debate. He took his M.A. degree by studying in his spare time and he had a very self-sacrificial attitude to life. In 1941 he married Alison Cree Brown, my wife's cousin, and after three and a half years as an officer in the New Zealand Expeditionary Force in jungle warfare against the Japanese, he was demobilised with the rank of captain. He has remained a loyal friend ever since.

Our last ten months in New Zealand were busy ones. After the summer missions and camps I embarked on a comprehensive tour of the whole country, visiting schools and speaking at farewell meetings. My theme on these occasions was 'Our future task — how shall we tackle it?' This was later printed and widely distributed. I finally handed over to Colin, fifteen years and five months since I first set foot in New Zealand. They had been wonderful years of growth and development with hundreds of warm-hearted friendships and hospitable homes and families. In the schools there were over seventy Crusader groups, a full programme of beach missions and camps in the school holidays, and some 20,000 members of the Scripture Union.

Colin Becroft, who had joined the staff in December 1938 was well qualified to lead the team of full-time field staff members which included, at that time, Margaret McGregor, with fourteen years 'on the road' to her credit, the Rev. Harry Thomson, southern district secretary and children's evangelist, Mary Thomson in Otago and Southland and Madge Logan as headquarters and editorial secretary. There was a well-staffed headquarters office and a bookshop and mail-order department, processing the sale of a full range of CSSM and SU publications, and evangelical literature imported from Britain and to a lesser extent from America. There was also an excellent council of men and women of wide experience who took a deep interest in all these developments and who met regularly to shape policy and give general guidance to the members of the staff.

What had been happening in New Zealand had been the local manifestation of what had now become a worldwide movement. In the providence of God it was a movement whose hour had come. Furthermore, New Zealand with its small population, at that time just over a million and a half, was sufficiently small to be influenced at a national level by our work. It was also a country with strong Christian traditions so that we had been reaping where others had sown.

On November 1st my wife and four children boarded the *Akaroa*. At last the actual moment of departure had come. A few friends came to see us off. The ship began to move and a gap appeared between us and the land. As I watched the strip of water slowly widen I felt a pang of regret. Now there was no turning back. It separated us from so much that we had loved and lived for, but it was no use brooding. Wellington Harbour, which is one of the most beautiful land-locked harbours in the world, was at its loveliest, but all too soon it disappeared behind the headland as we made for the open sea. We eventually reached our destination on December 13th at the port of Avonmouth on the Bristol Channel. There was no one to welcome us as the port was still out of bounds to the public. It was a bleak December day with overcast skies, and the wharves were littered with masses of broken concrete, twisted rusted iron and a few battered cranes. Everything looked grey, the sky, the sea, the leafless trees and even the slates on the roofs of the houses. Yet it all symbolised the brave resistance of the British people in their life and death struggle during the years of a terrible war. It was a moment of truth for me, for as a family we had escaped it all. The least we could do now was to play our part in helping to heal the nation's wounds and to aid in its reconstruction, based on reaching the new generation of the nation's youth with the healing and restoring power of the Gospel.

It was a few weeks after my fortieth birthday and as I stepped ashore I registered an inward resolve that come what may, I would see my new job through even if everything seemed to go wrong. It was a prophetic moment for it very nearly did go wrong, at least for a time.

We were taken by bus to Temple Meads Station in Bristol where Clarence Foster, our editorial secretary, was awaiting us and his loving welcome quickly made up for our dreary first impressions. We were soon on the train en-route for the little village of Kintbury, halfway between Bristol and London, where Dorothy Foster and some younger members of the family awaited us. The countryside was beautiful, covered with snow and gleaming in the winter sunshine. It was a wonderful welcome, and we were all happy together. Next day we caught the train from London to Glasgow and so to Kilmacolm where my father and my sisters Mona and Martha joyfully awaited us, while Nancy was still in Africa. There was one sad gap in our family for our devoted stepmother Nettie had died in August 1944.

8 RETURN TO ENGLAND

My ever-anxious father concerned about housing accommodation for us in the London area, had found a house which I was later able to buy from his friend W. W. Allen of Purley. We ourselves had planned to find accommodation in Ealing or North London but thankfully accepted the *fait accompli* and started to put down our roots in Surrey.

W. W. Allen was a leading elder at Montpelier Hall, now renamed Montpelier Church, and it was at this point that we had to decide where to place our church-going allegiance. We came to the conclusion that having committed ourselves to a course of action, we should not depart from it unless we had overwhelming guidance to make a change. This was a guiding principle in our association with the Brethren movement, and Montpelier Hall in particular.

On joining, I arranged a meeting with the elders to explain that I would be considerably occupied with Scripture Union work and would not be able to give much help in the affairs of the assembly and I asked if we could be accepted on that understanding. As time went on, however, I found myself able to serve as an elder for thirty years, and this was combined with preaching and pastoral responsibilities. We all shared in the various activities of our assembly life, and our four children were baptised by immersion on profession of faith. Eventually Graham, Margaret, and Elizabeth and their families found their fellowship in the Church of England, Janet married a Lutheran pastor and they made their home in Norway.

I do not think I could ever be a strong protagonist of any denomination or sect. I believe that the Brethren service of worship and of the Lord's supper is both right in principle and usually helpful in experience. But I have, when opportunities offered, taken communion in the Church of England, Presbyterian, Baptist and Lutheran churches. With regard to baptism, while I myself have been baptised by immersion, my wife, having been baptised in infancy in the Presbyterian church, does not feel the need for any further step and I quite appreciate her viewpoint. In public life, I have always tried most carefully to guard the reputation of the CSSM as a truly interdenominational society.

So, our life in England began. My wife found the adjustment painful although, true to her nature, she set about making a home for us all. Right at the start of our married life she had come to the conclusion that the only safe place to be is the one where the Lord has called. Consequently, despite the fact that she did not really want to leave her beloved New Zealand, deep down she felt that the Lord could not bless us if we stayed there. There was, however, an instinctive knowledge that somehow it was not going to be easy. She had visited England before for short periods and knew that although there was a warm and loving welcome from both my family and the Scripture Union family, there were many cultural differences. She became unsure of herself. She felt that she could not walk into a shop with any degree of confidence. The brands were different, the fish were different, even the cuts of meat had different names. And, in the South of England, even the names of the meals presented difficulties. Above all she felt that there were hidden taboos about what was 'done' and 'not done' and she couldn't seem to fathom what they were or why they were. It was only after several years that she finally said to herself, 'I must be myself. Our English friends must just accept me as I am.' And they did just that.

I myself felt this to a lesser extent and reacted by walking to the office in hot weather in my shirt sleeves and eating an ice cream in public. But slowly I began to conform and my dress, at any rate, was as British as the next man.

For the older children it wasn't easy either. Graham loved the outdoor life. In Wellington he could walk less than half a mile and fish off the jetty at Evans Bay. They could play outside after school for one or two hours, only coming in if it rained. And here we were, forty miles from the sea and no rivers in our part of Surrey either. And, to add to it all, school finished later and it got dark much earlier.

But there was, of course, a bright side. It was exciting to live in London where there was so much history to discover. Coming from New Zealand where a building a hundred years old was most unusual, the ancient architectural treasures were of particular interest, as were the great museums and art galleries. The nearness to the Continent meant that French, for instance, came to be a living reality and not just an academic exercise. So our horizons were widened, and as time went on we were greatly enriched by new friendships. Many of these were Scripture Union staff members from many countries who stayed in our home.

It was soon after our arrival in England that additional money came our way, this time from my father's side of the family. Grandfather Laird's business (John Laird & Son) had been taken over by E. S. and A. Robinson of Bristol, who specialised in packaging and paper. During the post-war years they began to prosper. Some of the shares in the company came our way and these increased greatly in value. This was quite an unexpected development and raised the question of the Christian ethics of inherited money. What should a Christian do? He could follow the noble example of D. E. Hoste of the CIM who, on receiving a legacy, gave it all away. But that meant that he was passing on the responsibility of administering it to someone else who might, or might not, do it well. I consulted a Quaker friend who said that the Friends did not mind some of their members being wealthy but they were concerned to see how well or badly they used their riches. The following Scriptures seemed relevant in the circumstances: '. . . if riches increase, set not your heart on them' (Psalm 62:10). And 'Do you seek great things for yourself? Seek them not . . .' (Jer. 45:5). To which may be added Lord Francis Bacon's wisdom: 'Seek not proud riches, but such as thou mayest get justly, use soberly, distribute cheerfully and leave contentedly.' (Essays Civil and Moral: xxxiv Of Riches.)

It was family money and our children would have a right to feel that some of the family patrimony should be handed on to them, and this was duly done. A proportion was put into a charitable trust and the annual refunds from the taxman generously augmented the funds available for distribution. We found that giving money away with a sense of responsibility was a pleasant but not by any means an easy task. One was in a favourable position to channel funds in strategic ways.

Sometimes it was a case of priming the pump, giving some new venture a start-off until such time as it had built up sufficient support to carry on. I was in a position to know where the shoe pinched especially in the evangelical world, and this was helpful in deploying the resources. One lesson learned from experience was that one of the best investments for dedicated money was in helping consecrated personalities.

In addition, I was able to serve for some years as general secretary in an honorary capacity. As our house was sufficiently large it was possible to give frequent hospitality, especially to overseas guests in the days when the international work of the Scripture Union was growing. Thus, one way or another, we accepted the gift of the stewardship of money and tried to make good use of the talents entrusted to us.

There is no doubt that trusts founded and administered by Christians have played an important role; yet much more could be done. Even a fairly small amount of money is all that is necessary for the formation of a private trust. Once having started a trust may well grow. The advice of a lawyer is essential, and there are a number of Christian legal firms who have wide experience in trust work of this kind.

On December 31st, 1947, our fifth child was born. It was an easy birth but before long my wife began to wonder if something was wrong. Then Dr. Binning, our family doctor, told me one Saturday morning in the kindliest way that our little son was not normal and that he should be seen by a specialist. He said that the easy birth was partly because his skull was soft and that there was a serious abnormality.

In those days we used to have large reunion meetings in the Central Hall, Westminster, when children, leaders and workers from beach missions and camps would gather for a large inspirational rally. On this Saturday afternoon I was the main speaker and gave a lecture on Bunyan's *Pilgrim's Progress* illustrated by coloured lantern slides. It was very hard to keep my mind on the subject. Every now and then the thought intruded: 'When I get home I have to break the news to Marion.'

At last it was over and I was by her bedside. She took the news with great courage and without bitterness or rebellion. We could only try to believe that we had been entrusted with

105

this little life to care for, that we could do this as a family group, and this is how it came about. Alistair was beloved by us all. He was a sweet-natured child and responded to music. But his head was so large that he could hardly hold it up, an unusual form of hydrocephaly due to a developmental defect similar in principle to spina bifida.

When he was about three years old we were faced with an acutely painful dilemma. The poor little boy had difficulty in breathing as the space in the upper part of his throat became more and more restricted. His sleep and ours was increasingly disturbed by his tendency to choke. Broken nights and family responsibilities bore down heavily and we reluctantly began to wonder if it would be necessary to have him looked after in some suitable care centre, at least on a part-time basis. At that time, just after the war, very little help was available either from the hospitals or in the way of voluntary organisations. We made enquiries but these were fruitless. Today, help would have come from a number of voluntary organisations but we knew of none in 1950.

It did not seem to us to be a case for invoking the words of James, Chapter 5, in relation to the prayer for healing, but rather that we should put our trust in God and humbly accept what He had allowed, doing what seemed best for the little boy himself and for the other members of the family. We were very conscious of the love, prayers and sympathy of our many friends and our fellow church members. This in itself was a healing ministry without any special 'ceremony'. We just knew that we were being upheld.

I seriously wondered if the time might come when it would seem right to give up my job with Scripture Union and devote myself to the care of similarly handicapped children.

We did not try to search for a meaning. This was hidden from us at the time but now, after the lapse of many years, we can truthfully say that it was an experience for which we could only be thankful. It was as if the Lord was saying: 'Here is this little boy, I want you to look after him for me and I will give you the strength.'

When Alistair was three years and nine months old we were at our wits' end. And then, and not before, he died leaving behind a memory of a deeply-loved and sweet-natured child.

It was an experience which enriched each member of our family, and gave some insight into God's mysterious ways. It left my wife and me with a very deep awareness of other parents and families whose trials with a handicapped child have been deeper and far longer lasting than ours. The care of a Mongol child, a prolonged mental illness or the care of a hopelessly senile parent: all these were brought home to us with a far greater compassion. Perhaps Mother Teresa's phrase, popularised by Malcolm Muggeridge, 'Something beautiful for God', may point to a clue.

I have asked my wife Marion for her assessment of this traumatic event in our lives and this is what she says:

I was asked how I felt when I knew Alistair was not normal. I don't know. I am not good at defining my feelings. I remember saying to John that I could take it if people did not express sympathy; I would break down if they did. I think what ran through my mind was the people I had known with such children: the woman in my home town in New Zealand with a spina bifida daughter who wheeled her about in a bed on wheels, and I remember my father saying that she had devoted her life to that child. Then there was Billy, the Mongol boy who, when the pipe band or the Salvation Army marched, swung along beside them or in front of them, beating time with a stick: the picture of enjoyment. I also remembered a fellow church member tied to a cerebro-spastic daughter in a wheelchair (I admired that woman immensely), and my own little spina bifida brother who lived only one month. But I believed that whatever lay ahead, God would surely give the strength needed.

People vary so much in their reactions to such a situation. I left Alistair in the pram outside a shop on one occasion and when I came out, two friends were peering into the pram but on seeing me they jumped back and talked about something different. They just didn't know what to say.

There were those who said that we should put a child like Alistair into care straight away for the sake of the other children. But we felt that however inscrutable God's ways are to us, He does not make mistakes, and that there

107

was something for us in this experience which would be irrevocably lost if we handed Alistair over to care. In fact we are certain that our family gained an understanding of others in misfortune. Years later, one of our daughters said that if we had put Alistair into care it would have had a very bad effect for she would have felt we could do the same to her.

The youngest child, Elizabeth, just four years older, hardly realised that anything was wrong with him. She and Janet would take him for a walk in the pram sometimes. I asked if they minded. 'Oh no,' they said, 'if people stare, we just stare back.' To the oldest girl, Margaret, he was someone special. She would come in from school, scoop him up off the floor and dance around the kitchen with him in her arms singing, 'My baby, my baby.' After he died she could not bring herself to mention his name for years. We used to take him to church and leave him sleeping in the pram, and after the service she would stand with the pram while people hung over the other babies, and no one took any notice of Alistair. Of course they didn't know what to say, but her attitude was that they could at least say what lovely hair he had or what lovely blue eyes he had, which was true.

There were several babies of similar age at the church. On one Sunday we had a quite outstanding morning service and after it four babies were dedicated. As I looked at those beautiful babies brought down to the front with their parents it was suddenly too much. I could not have sat there with Alistair. It would have been trying for the other parents and the church as a whole, I felt. Alistair was wholly the Lord's as far as we were concerned, but the realisation that he was so different engulfed me and I had to go out. A friend followed me and tried to comfort me. 'It has brought out the best in the other children,' she said, and I think she was right.

Years later, when our daughter Janet was a worker at a seaside mission a family came with a child seriously incapacitated and she offered to wheel her about while the mother went into the service for once with her husband and son. The mother demurred until Janet said, 'I had a brother like this. I understand.'

On one occasion Graham came across a photograph of Alistair in a medical text-book. It was quite a shock. But on reflection he had a feeling of thankfulness that the medical condition (oxycephaly) of his little brother, whose arrival he had looked forward to so keenly, was in some small way being used to help students and doctors to understand other cases of this kind.

We felt that it was better for our children to face reality. In our modern welfare state the sick, crippled, derelict and handicapped are seldom seen in our streets or homes. For the most part they are tidily screened within the walls of hospitals and other institutions. Thus a misleading picture is given of general well-being, disguising the more distressing realities of our common humanity.

On one occasion, a senior woman in the church invited me to lunch with Alistair and encouraged me to talk. I think she wanted to know how we were coping and how the children were reacting. I remember saying that I didn't think I could watch him die. 'You may not have to,' she said.

When that time did come his breathing was very distressing. He would fall asleep in my arms and then wake up clutching me with the fear of choking. John was booked for meetings in Manchester and Liverpool, and we agreed that he should carry on with these, but arrangements were made for a night nurse during his absence as I had four other children and badly needed sleep.

At five a.m. on the morning of September 29th, 1951, the nurse called me to say that she thought he was unconscious. The doctor came and gave him an injection but he never regained consciousness. John cancelled his meetings and was home a few hours later. The newspaper announcement quoted the words of I Corinthians 15:43, 'Sown in weakness . . . raised in power.'

It is the little things one remembers. One sunny morning we put a barricade at the front door steps so that Alistair could enjoy the sunshine. A fox terrier appeared and barked at him, surprised perhaps at seeing such an unusual looking child. He laughed and laughed and the more he laughed the more the dog barked.

On Sunday nights after tea we all used to gather round the piano to sing hymns, each one choosing their own hymn. Our youngest daughter chose the same hymn each Sunday for months: 'Children of Jerusalem Sang the praise of Jesu's name', with the catchy, repetitive chorus: 'Hark! Hark! Hark! While infant voices sing Loud hosannas to our king.'

Alistair loved this tune. He would sit propped against a cushion, fingering a hymn book with a look of eager expectancy. At odd times throughout the week he would hum that tune, never right through, but he knew it all. Years later at a service it was announced as the children's hymn and I suddenly found myself too choked to sing it.

As the years have passed I can honestly say that the memories of the difficulties and the hardness of the way have faded. It is the poignant things and the happy things that remain.

9 GENTLEMEN OF LONDON

My first impression of the offices at Wigmore Street was the council room which served the double purpose of being both council room and my office. The windows overlooked the busy Wigmore Street traffic. On my desk there lay a pad of clean pink blotting-paper. A solidly built council table occupied the centre of the room and a pleasant coal fire flanked by two large leather chairs, kept out the January cold.

The walls were hung with large photographs in heavy frames of the founding fathers of the CSSM. Josiah Spiers with his bushy beard, his hooked nose and bright eyes, T. B. Bishop, Henry Hankinson, Henry Hutchinson and Edwin Arrowsmith. To me they were a reminder of the past rather than an inspiration for the future. Much as I respected and admired them for the great work they did in the early days, I felt that the emphasis was not quite what was wanted for 1946. Gradually one after another found their way on to the walls of the corridors and eventually down to the basement. They were replaced by a number of landscape reproductions. One, however, did remain, and that was T. B. Bishop who, for fifty-two years, had served as the honorary secretary of the CSSM and the Scripture Union. The story of his life is told in *TBB of the CSSM*, now long out of print. Born in London in 1839 the son of a Hampshire farmer, he became honorary secretary in 1868 at the age of 29. He capably fulfilled his daily work at the Customs House and spent the rest of his time at the office, then in the City at 13a Warwick Lane, where he sometimes worked until eleven p.m. He was a cautious and conservative man, but he always kept a strong sense of humour. He never used the telephone ('I don't like it. It's alive!'). He did not marry until he was fifty-eight but when he did it was a very happy match. In later life he became increasingly conservative and opposed the introduction of Scripture Union notes, considering the reading cards quite adequate.

I also admired the man for his practical attitude to finance in connection with the Lord's work. In the missionary world of the nineteen thirties, some years after TBB's death in 1920, there was a strong emphasis on the work and ideals of the 'faith' missions, some of which were idealistic but sometimes impractical. They had a big casualty list with missionaries returning home disillusioned after a short period of service. There was a certain amount of irresponsibility on the part of some mission boards for the rehabilitation of the casualities and the care of the sick, aged and widows. These missionaries were expected to look to the Lord in faith for the provision of all their needs. Reports were given of the encouragements and victories but the failures and tragedies were seldom mentioned or only hinted at. One missionary serving in India, and well-known to me, had no monthly remittance for four months. He had to live off the land as best he could and had no money, not even enough to buy a stamp to send a letter to his fiancée. Others were so poor that they had to use sacking for window curtains. One missionary family working in South America had to subsist on a diet of potatoes for some weeks.

Some of the best, notably the China Inland Mission (now OMF) combined the 'faith' principle with the practical care of the missionaries' children, the old people and the sick. They looked to the Lord and were mighty in prayer and faith but they also looked for help, both financial and otherwise, from their prayer partners. They produced attractive literature and appointed home directors who kept the needs of the mission field well to the fore. Missionaries on the field were given guidance and pastoral care by field directors. Like George Müller, they combined the miraculous with the strictly practical.

In general the 'faith missions' tended to be regarded as more spiritual, and perhaps indeed they were, but some of them were seriously lacking in responsible wisdom and common sense. However, in recent years there have been much more realistic developments and there are fewer cases of severe and unnecessary hardship. The early founders of the CSSM faced the dilemma as to whether to look to the Lord alone, or to make the needs known and even appeal for funds.

They began on the strictly 'faith' principle, but, along with a number of other infant societies, they nearly perished. There were anxious consultations about the gas bill, and the committee members had to help out from their own bank accounts.

Then T. B. Bishop became honorary secretary. The policy was carefully reviewed and a statement was drawn up and agreed, to the effect that while trusting the Lord, they might also look to the Lord's people for the financial help needed in bringing the message of the Gospel to the children. This has been the policy ever since. The main difference in viewpoint could be illustrated by reference to the examples of Hudson Taylor on the one hand and D. L. Moody on the other. The CIM under the leadership of Hudson Taylor illustrated the 'faith' principle at its best. D. L. Moody, the practical, down-to-earth, mid-Western American had no compunction about taking up offerings at his meetings and appealing for money for his many projects. He would even call on wealthy Christians and ask straight out for a large donation.

I was surprised to find how much people in office jobs wrote letters to each other. In Wellington we would lift the telephone and talk, but at Wigmore Street the various departmental heads would write letters to a large number of correspondents on all manner of subjects. This great tradition of letter writing was carried over from the Victorian era, and Mr. Hubbard and my colleague, Clarence Foster, were masters of the art.

J. H. Hubbard had a small team of highly trained secretaries, who had learned his style of writing and knew how his mind worked. They would compose and type (or dictate to a junior) his letters for signature at the end of each day. In this way the frail little man from his office in London, built up a network of Scripture Union secretaries, staff members and personal friends all over the world. I was at the receiving end in New Zealand for many years, and his letters from London, some of which I still keep, played an important part in my decision to give up medicine and join the staff. He used to say to me, 'Write to them, John, as if they were your dearest friend.' And that was how he wrote to me in my student days in the

113

1920s, and until I went to London in 1946, invariably signing himself 'Yours affectionately'.

However there can be no substitute for the personal interview, and in dealing with delicate situations the letter can have severe limitations. On one occasion I had to deal with a colleague on a sensitive issue and I wrote him a letter which I thought was a model of tact and understanding. A few days later I had a very pained telephone call from him asking if he could come and see me. I then found that my letter had reached him and had been read by him at two a.m. on his return home from an exhausting weekend of meetings and personal counselling. It had worried him so much that he had hardly slept for the rest of the night, but as we talked it was an easy matter to clear up the misunderstanding. I was only sorry that I had not arranged for a personal talk in the first instance.

In January 1946, the CSSM council consisted of sixteen members, thirteen of whom attended fairly regularly. They were nearly all professional men with a preponderance of lawyers, secretaries and accountants, all working in the City. The average age was about fifty-eight and of these one was in the thirties age bracket, six were in the fifties age bracket, six were in the sixties, two in their seventies and one over eighty. They were nearly all successful men in their own spheres and most were quite well-off financially. They were united in their love for the CSSM and in their desire for its welfare and effectiveness, and they combined spiritual qualities with a good measure of common sense.

On the whole our council was a good one and would have compared favourably with similar councils in London at the time. Its members had been carefully chosen, they inherited a long and honourable history and the CSSM was something very precious to them. Montague Goodman used to say, 'I am a child of the CSSM', and Frank Bacon said several times, 'The CSSM is the best loved society in England.' They understood its importance in the life of the nation, in the lives of countless boys and girls, and adults, at home and abroad, and they wanted to be quite sure that they were putting its interests first. They were gentlemen of England, or more accurately, gentlemen of London. After all, London was then the heart of the Empire and, to a large extent, the business centre of the world.

The council met once a month over coffee and sandwiches, the proceedings were dignified and pleasant, and the members were addressed by the chairman as 'Gentlemen'. No one dreamed that the day would come when there would be clergymen and ladies on the council as there are now. There was seldom any sense of urgency, and business could usually be deferred if time ran out. Delays of a month, or even months, were of little consequence.

As in most councils of any size, there was a small inner core who carried the main burden. In this case there were two who fulfilled this role and who worked closely together, A. B. Keith, the chairman, and his friend Frank D. Bacon.

I stood somewhat in awe of the London council, and to some extent of Clarence who was thirteen years older than me. I regarded them as my 'elders and betters', and it was not quite the done thing to question their wisdom, at least outwardly. There was one occasion when one of our colleagues registered a mild protest against a council decision. When this was discussed in a council meeting Mr. Montague Goodman exclaimed in a tone of slight indignation, 'But, Mr. Chairman, they are our servants!'.

Mr. Hubbard had persuaded Mr. Keith to give him full council membership, which put him in a strong position for he was also the secretary to the council and produced the agendas and the minutes.

My own view has always been that the chief executive of a religious or charitable organisation should not be a member of its governing council, because the council members in their primary function as trustees should be detached from personal financial interests, and should be free if necessary to dismiss or otherwise discipline the paid members of the staff. Neither Clarence nor I expected to be given council membership and needless to say the council did not suggest it.

Owing to age and infirmity Mr. Hubbard was unable to give a strong lead, but at the same time it seems that he could not bear the thought of retirement. While on the one hand he seemed keen to have me on the staff, he was emotionally reluctant to hand over responsibility. This may have accounted for the vagueness of his letters to me while in New Zealand. He continued to be secretary to the council after I arrived, and to write the minutes until his final retirement in September 1946. He should therefore have been the sole and official channel of communication between the council and myself but, as already noted, I received communications from three sources, Mr. Keith, Mr. Hubbard and Clarence, each with a different emphasis. The result was vagueness and confusion of which I was not aware at the time and only came to realise in retrospect.

There did not appear to have been much co-ordination between Mr. Hubbard and Clarence, for during the war-years Mr. Hubbard had his office at Chesham, twenty-six miles to the north of London, and Clarence was at Kintbury, sixty-three miles to the west. They probably communicated by letter as occasion required or at a council meeting in London.

Clarence returned to London in January 1946 but Mr. Hubbard continued to operate from his war-time offices in Chesham, where he dealt with his extensive correspondence at home and abroad. After six months I very reluctantly pointed this out to the council who appointed a committee of two, Mr. Montague Goodman and Mr. Frank Bacon, to interview Mr. Hubbard and to ask for his formal retirement. Mr. Bacon did not attend the meeting and Mr. Goodman had the painful task of asking the good old man to give up the work he loved. I found this a very painful episode. It was only then that the full overseas correspondence came into my hands.

Clarence Foster was a man of quiet faith, prayer and spiritual discernment, and with a mind well-stored with Scripture.

He was unable to speak at public meetings or even conduct general office prayers, owing to a feeling of nervousness which overcame him. He had, however, in his younger days led a CSSM with his brother Godfrey and had been a good speaker. By temperament he was more of a trustee than a leader, a man of the old school concerned to preserve the proprieties and traditions of the Mission in which he had served as editorial secretary since 1922.

About nine o'clock each morning my colleagues and I disappeared into our various offices and only referred to one another when some specific subject had to be discussed. I

116

tentatively suggested that we should have a weekly meeting with the heads of the departments, but this was not approved, mainly on the grounds that we were all too busy with our jobs, but also perhaps because it had never been done before. I then suggested that we should meet once a week for prayer. This was reluctantly agreed to, but the meeting was poorly attended and there was doubt as to who should lead it. Clarence and I were supposed to take turns but we sometimes forgot whose turn it was! Our colleagues had to wait patiently while this was discussed and decided.

In some ways we were complimentary to each other, but in another sense our outlook on life in general was very different. Clarence sought for quietness and tranquillity and looked to the past, while I looked to the future and knew myself to be involved, not always successfully, in the struggles of the spiritual battlefield.

In 1946 when we were appointed as the two secretaries of the Mission, Clarence became secretary to the council following Mr. Hubbard's retirement, and prepared the agendas and wrote the minutes, a task I gladly left to him. But it meant that all new suggestions and proposals had to be channelled through him, and this sometimes led to delays and frustrations.

He was on the council of a number of well-known evangelical organisations, such as Keswick, IVF, London Bible College, and was also vice-president and joint treasurer of Cambridge Inter-Collegiate Christian Union. Naturally these took up a certain amount of his time. It might have been thought that Clarence would automatically succeed Mr. Hubbard, but his gifts were really more suited to working, to use one of his favourite phrases, 'behind the scenes'. One can well understand that the council would wish to honour him for his long and faithful service, and the idea of a joint secretaryship with myself would seem to be an ideal solution, especially as both he and I were quite happy with the arrangement initially.

During the war-years Hubert Smith had conducted the business affairs of the Mission from the offices at 5 Wigmore Street. On more than one occasion fire bombs had landed on the roof, and had been promptly extinguished by him and his fire-watching team.

Although I never received any letters from him while I was still in New Zealand, I soon realised that he had played an important part in general policy making, especially as he could make his views known to the council through the medium of his friend Frank Bacon, who had stood by him and helped him so loyally during the war-years.

His father before him had been a village evangelist with the Caravan Mission to Village Children (a subsidiary of the Children's Special Service Mission), and he had joined the staff at the old office at 13A Warwick Lane on June 1st, 1921, at a commencing salary of £250 p.a. The official office hours were nine to six with the usual half-holiday on Saturday and a fortnight's holiday in the summer. For the next thirty-six years he devoted himself completely to his tasks, working long hours in the evenings and sometimes over the weekend. Having been in charge during the war he naturally found it difficult to adjust to the coming of Clarence and myself as his seniors, especially as no decision had been made as to whether he was to be responsible to Clarence or to me. He was therefore free to choose which of us he preferred to consult, which made it all too easy to play one of us off against the other, but for the rest he ruled his own well-established kingdom. At one time he asked the council if he could be given the title of general manager but this was declined — it was a decision which hurt him deeply. Unable to delegate he tried to work harder and harder to keep up with the growing volume of work, and his desk was always smothered in papers. He used to say, 'Dr. Laird, this place is built on detail.' How right he was! When he retired after an extension at his own request of a year or two beyond the age of sixty-five, he never crossed our threshold again. He took over the management of the Evangelical Literature Trust Bookshop in Bristol, where he kept busy and found some happiness. He was a man of few words and behind his quiet manner there was gold deep down, which I only gradually discovered. When he died in August 1976 I was deeply touched to find that he had made me the first-named executor of his Will, for we had had many battles on matters of policy. Even from his modest estate he left a generous proportion to the Mission he had served so long and faithfully.

Another personality for special mention is that of the Rev. E. J. H. Nash. I soon realised that his programme of Varsities and Public School Camps and houseparties for schoolboys was of unique importance. From time to time I heard criticisms, both at council meetings and elsewhere, to the effect that 'Bash', as he was affectionately known, was specialising too exclusively in recruiting boys from thirty of England's more famous elitist schools. It was also said that he exercised too strong an influence over his campers' lives, for instance, in their choice of career and in pledging their loyalty first and foremost to 'camp', and all that it stood for.

I took an early opportunity of visiting Eric Nash in his own surroundings. It was not a canvas camp but was set in a handsome country house used by the 'campers' during the school holidays. In term-time it was a boys' boarding school and was situated near a little village with the intriguing name of Iwerne Minster in a beautiful part of Dorset about twenty miles from the sea. I was given a friendly welcome and quickly sensed the relaxed and normal atmosphere. I found Bash to be a thoughtful man with an air of quiet confidence, wholly dedicated to his task of helping to bring boys and young men to a personal faith in Christ and to a life of complete dedication to His service. He was of slender build, not athletic, with a dignified, slightly reserved manner. His dark eyebrows, quiet eyes and regular features gave the impression of serenity, balanced with a strong sense of humour. No one loved a funny story more than Bash, and if the atmosphere became too solemn he would break in with some cheerful nonsense or impish teasing. His talks at camp prayers were simple and relevant, but his main strength and effectiveness was in his pastoral care of young converts, and his training of the camp officers in personal evangelism. He would travel long distances to help a small group of Christians in a boarding school and follow up with letters and suggestions for guided reading.

Boys would join the Scripture Union and were provided with specially written Scripture Union notes. The long-term result of this careful work was that a steady stream of intel-ligent and capable men found their way into the universities, the church, the teaching profession, and other leadership positions in public life.

The pattern was reminiscent of the ministry of William Orange of New Zealand, and I could not help but warm to the man and his work. One of his colleagues wrote that,

> He has always been a quiet man, in voice, manner and dress. His favourite milieu has not been the pulpit or the platform, but rather the sitting-room of some under-graduate, a housemaster's drawing-room, or the library of Iwerne Minster. It is here, in a quiet, persuasive and penetrating way that he has carried the Gospel message to the hearts of innumerable young people. Very few men in our day have touched the springs of so many lives, and to very few can so many have dared 'to unlock the heart and let it speak'.

While we were not uncritical of some aspects of his work, Clarence and I, and increasingly the council, decided to back him with such financial and moral support as he might need. Bash is now in his eighties and, having handed over the leadership to others, he carries on in his quiet and imperturb-able way, well content to see many of his spiritual children and children's children growing in spiritual maturity.

Early in 1946 Mr. Hubbard invited me to go with him on his annual pilgrimage to Cambridge and later to Oxford. We stayed at the best hotels with a private sitting-room where we interviewed undergraduates as possible leaders and workers at seaside missions for the following summer. The links between the CSSM and CICCU (Cambridge Inter-Collegiate Christian Union) were very strong dating back to 1885 when Edwin Arrowsmith, a CSSM staff member, recruited beach mission workers from Cambridge and, to a lesser extent, from Oxford.

After Mr. Hubbard had retired I continued this tradition of talent scouting. Years before Paul White had introduced me to the idea of keeping a prayer list of up-and-coming men. He called it his BWW list, Blokes Worth Watching! My BWW list of those years included Frederick Catherwood, for three years a camp officer, now Sir Frederick Catherwood, a well-known Christian industrialist, John Stott of All Soul's, Langham Place, a leading camp officer at Iwerne Minster; and Michael Griffiths, later general director of the Overseas Missionary Fellowship and now Principal of the London Bible College, a former leader at Abersoch CSSM. These and many others were indeed Blokes Worth Watching and praying for!

As a Mission we had the great advantage of possessing the Wigmore Street building which, despite opposition from the council, had been planned by Mr. Hubbard in the 1920s and saved from destruction by Hubert Smith during the war. In 1946 this building housed an administrative and clerical staff of about fifty, most of whom were in Hubert Smith's department.

Harold Ling was our accountant and assistant to the secretaries, and R. T. Garwood was the secretary of the Caravan Mission to Village Children. Soon others joined us, Reginald Hill as secretary for Sunday Schools, Morgan Derham as editorial secretary, Quintin Carr as secretary for camps and seaside missions, assisted by Mary Ellis for girls' camps, and Branse Burbridge for the Inter-School Christian Fellowship. Quintin was rather a special friend as we had worked together in Glasgow in the 1920s when he was a student at the Bible Training Institute and I was at Glasgow University. We helped to look after a group of boys who met in Glasgow High School, a group which may well have been a forerunner of similar school Christian Unions in Scotland and many other countries.

During the war the field work at home and abroad had been carried on in spite of difficulties. In the summer of 1945 twenty-three seaside missions had been arranged, and thirty-four camps and house-parties, largely staffed by voluntary workers. The Caravan Mission to Village Children, with twenty-one evangelists, was at work in twenty-eight counties, while a limited number of children's missions had been led by a small number of full-time children's evangelists.

Paper shortages had reduced the output of Scripture Union notes, magazines and books and a skeleton service had survived but, despite the difficulties, hundreds of Scripture Union honorary secretaries continued their valuable work.

In countries such as Switzerland, Australia and New Zealand the war had had a stimulating effect, while India and South Africa had been only slightly affected. But in the war zones on the European continent our work had been almost extinguished.

10   JOINT SECRETARYSHIP

When we were in England in 1939 for the Diamond Jubilee
meetings I had been asked to consider an invitation to join the
staff at Wigmore Street in a year or two's time, war-time
conditions permitting. My first reaction had been quite
favourable, especially as I warmly welcomed the opportunity
of working in close fellowship with Clarence Foster whose
kindliness and fellowship were so evident.

During the next few years a friendly but rather vague
correspondence continued. Sometimes Clarence Foster would
write, sometimes Mr. Hubbard, but although the letters were
cordial it was not clear what my future role would be.

Towards the end of 1942 I received a letter from Mr. A. B.
Keith to say that he had been elected chairman of the London
council. He continued:

> The question of a successor to Mr. Hubbard is very much in
> all our minds for he is getting on in years (he is nearly
> seventy-one and a half) and cannot be expected to carry on
> much longer. In addition, the post-war period, I feel, will
> require new methods and a wider outlook and one cannot
> expect old hands to face up to all this. I have had many talks
> with the members of the council and they are all, without
> exception, hoping that you will be led of God to come here
> after the war to accept the post of general secretaryship . . .
> I believe Hubbard wrote to you suggesting a period of
> 'learning' under him but this is not my idea of the procedure
> at all. If you come home, I would like you to 'take over'
> entirely with the help of such members of staff who have
> various duties . . . We are all praying much that you will be
> guided of God and we are hoping that He will lead you to
> come home and help us in this wonderful CSSM work.

This all seemed very much to the point; but as time went on
the suggestion emerged in the course of correspondence with

123

Clarence Foster that there should be a joint secretaryship as between Clarence and myself.

My respect for the London council was such that I adhered to their judgment in this as in other matters, and in January 1943 gave my cordial consent to whatever arrangements they might think best in the circumstances, with the single proviso that I would be free from detailed office work.

Later it was suggested that Clarence and I should be associated together in the secretarial work of the Mission and that, if possible, a third man should be appointed as assistant to the secretaries.

During this period, Clarence and I continued to correspond intermittently. He wrote long letters full of warmth and friendliness and with many expressions of hope and expectations and trust in God. They dealt mainly with affairs at London headquarters, and had frequent references for the need for prayer and being led step by step. He repeatedly said how much he was looking forward to our working together; how Mr. Hubbard was now seventy-three and sometimes unwell; how the council was out of touch with the realities of the situation and how Hubert Smith, our business manager, was taking increasing control and wanted to be given the title of general manager.

He reported early in 1944 that a secretarial committee had been set up to arrange for the conduct of secretarial duties in Wigmore Street. He wrote:

> It is pathetic in many ways to see how little our council members here really know about the work. The result is that a good deal is said and done in council meetings concerning which one scarcely knows whether to laugh or weep. I am more and more persuaded that the whole system is antiquated and in urgent need of some kind of revision . . . As far as I can see, the only solution lies in the council being willing to give a little more executive authority to the men they entrust with the leadership of the work. As you know, the plan is that you and I are to be joint secretaries. The thought in the mind of the council is that you will carry on what is so urgently needed, and that which is upon your own heart, i.e. the 'inspirational' ministry, infusing new spiritual

life into all the activities of the Mission both at headquarters and over the country. Then the council want you to take charge of our overseas work, as far as that can be done from London, and also the oversight of the seaside and camp arrangements. I gather that I am to be more responsible for the Scripture Union work and possibly the home staff workers, but I visualise a joint partnership with mutual confidence and conference regarding all these matters.

In a subsequent letter (5.12.44), I replied: 'One thing is absolutely clear to me that the mutual trust and confidence between you and me is on a very secure footing and I really cannot imagine anything which would shake it, though there again it is extraordinary how the devil can gain an advantage by subtle methods; so we will definitely be on our guard against any such subtle attacks.'

Unfortunately, our 'mutual trust and confidence' was to be severely shaken. One is reminded of the fable that a day came when the devil decided to go out of business. He sold all his tools, but one tool he could not bring himself to part with, and that was a wedge, his most effective weapon. The day came when that wedge was driven deeply between the two of us. But never to breaking point.

Our chairman, Mr. Keith, was unwell when I arrived from New Zealand, but he invited me to visit him at his home in Sevenoaks. He was kindness itself, but I gained little light on the role I was expected to fulfil, or the precise relationship that should exist between my senior colleagues and myself. Thus the vagueness which had characterised much of the earlier correspondence continued. No reference was made to his letter to me of December 1942, in which he had said, 'The members of the council are, without exception, hoping that you will be led of God to come here after the war to accept the post of general secretary', and I didn't mention it either. It must be said here how much we are the children of our times. In those days it was not 'the gentlemanly thing' to push oneself forward. I had been brought up on the principle of respecting and even revering my leaders, and in the early days in London it hardly occurred to me to question their decisions, though inwardly I was sometimes confused and apprehensive.

All Mr. Keith would say was that Clarence and I were to be put on a level as the two joint secretaries and the council would watch to see which of us 'emerged', and that he hoped it would be me! Some months later, when walking in the country with Montague Goodman, one of our senior council members, he too remarked that Clarence and I were to be on an equal footing, but it was expected that one of us would 'emerge', and that he too hoped it would be me. I asked, 'Does Clarence know this?' After some hesitation he replied, 'Not exactly.'

With my Brethren background the idea of informal, emergent leadership was quite familiar and acceptable. In support of this concept half a sentence from the authorised version of the Bible, Proverbs 18:16, was sometimes quoted: 'A man's gift maketh room for him.' This was thought to mean that a man, gifted by the Holy Spirit with leadership, teaching, or some other quality, would have his gift recognised by common consent, and he would be able to exercise his ministry in the Assembly. But on closer examination the whole sentence reads: 'A man's gift maketh room for him and bringeth him before great men.' When compared with modern translations it appears that the 'gift' is not a gift conferred by the Holy Spirit in a New Testament sense, but a gift of money or something valuable to smooth the way and gain acceptance with 'great men'; in other words, a bribe! This is one example of the undue influence which can be exercised by a telling phrase misconstrued and taken out of its context. It is not the only one of its kind; the power of the slogan in the secular world has its counterparts in the religious scene, though perhaps in milder forms. At the January council meeting in 1946, which Mr. Keith was unable to attend, it was decided, under Mr. Bacon's chairmanship, that our titles would simply be 'secretaries of the CSSM and Scripture Union'.

One disadvantage of this became immediately apparent. It meant that no one person had responsibility under the council for the welfare and leadership of the organisation as a whole, but I did not realise this at the time. We were to be departmental secretaries and nothing more.

Yet only close supervision by one person charged with overall responsibility could adequately meet a constantly changing situation. Because human situations are never static, leadership and administration are never static. We have to go on reorganising all the time. No sooner has an arrangement been made than a valued colleague leaves, new appointments are made, new developments are entered upon or some projects die away. There may be crises of one kind or another which cannot wait for the next council meeting. Lists of responsibilities and duties, organisation charts, job specifications are all useful, but seldom a month goes by before they have to be changed or modified. We were not dealing with rigid structures of brick or stone, but with men and women who themselves had their problems and whose relationships were constantly changing.

I came to realise increasingly that leadership is a continuous process. The living organism has to be controlled, adjusted and pruned, petty quarrels have to be settled and misunderstandings cleared up. There has to be comfort in sorrow, erring brethren called to order, tardy brethren stimulated and the over-zealous restrained.

None of these things can be done by a council because they cannot be present as a body at any given moment when they are needed. For them, the unit of time is usually the month, but for the executive the unit of time is sometimes even a minute. The long distance phone call comes through and a decision or advice has to be given immediately. A worried colleague knocks at the door and needs help, not next week, but now. An overseas visitor calls without an appointment and must be seen at once.

A further difficulty about the council's proposals was that they were vague, over-simplified and inadequate. They did not and could not take into account the fact that we had to deal with complex situations and complex personalities. Only an exhaustive analysis by someone experienced in the skills of management could do this adequately, so we had to put up with a very amateurish, though well-intentioned allocation of duties, in which there were many hidden ambitions for status, titles, responsibilities or lack of them. To spot the sources of trouble required a diagnostic skill of a high order, to be followed by the right treatment. But we had two people 'in charge', each of whom had quite different ways of dealing

127

with the problems as they arose. Consequently the staff were confused and comparisons were inevitably made.

There were times when I felt that the council or church elders or some other committee under which I have served have been the graveyard of many hopes and plans. Nothing is easier than for a committee to say 'wait', or 'some day perhaps' or 'no'. On the other hand there have been great moments when a council has really found its soul and, refusing to wait for the tardy brethren, has given a lead in some great project. I can recall occasions when the CSSM council was faced with what seemed to be an insuperable problem. Before the meetings began I could not imagine how a solution could be found. Yet when it was all over and the captains and the kings had departed, leaving the general secretary and occasionally the chairman lingering for a few precious minutes among the coffee cups and papers, we could only utter a prayer of deep thanksgiving that the way forward had, as by a miracle of divine mercy, been made clear.

When the time came in later years to research the actual minutes, it became even more apparent that the council had had great difficulty in apportioning the duties and responsibilities to the two secretaries. The matter would be discussed, sometimes by the council as a whole, sometimes by the general purposes and finance committee and, on a number of occasions, by a special secretarial committee which had been set up for the purpose.

From time to time different conclusions were reached. For instance it was suggested that I should be responsible for the overseas work and Clarence for the work in the home country. Or that Clarence should be responsible for the Scripture Union and I for the CSSM. One suggestion was that there should be four secretaries, a home secretary, a foreign secretary, a literature secretary and a camps secretary, but without any mention of a general secretary to co-ordinate their activities. In the course of these researches I found that the constitution of the Mission under its Articles of Association required that there should be, 'a) One chief secretary who shall be appointed and removed only by the society in general meeting. The first chief secretary shall be Mr. Tom Bond Bishop. b) One or more other secretaries.' But this requirement had been lost sight of until long after the joint secretaryship had become the established status quo. On one occasion Mr. Keith remarked, 'The council is going to be the general secretary'! This may not have been intended to be taken too seriously, but it did seem to betray a misunderstanding as to the proper functions of a council, which are mainly those of trusteeship and broad policy making rather than executive action.

A year or two later I raised the question of the joint secretaryship with Mr. Goodman. He said enigmatically, 'Nothing can be done about it now.' As he left the room my heart sank and a feeling of despair came over me. The irony of it was that I was given to understand from Clarence that he too had been told by one council member that one day he would be general secretary to the Mission.

But at the time we both accepted the position, on the surface at any rate. I supposed that as I was the new boy I needed to be tested. But for how long? Surely after a year some decision or clarification would be made. I did not guess that ten years were to elapse before my 'probationary' period would be over.

I once ventured to ask Frank Bacon what the council thought of me. 'Young man in a hurry', was the laconic reply. It hurt. Some words of appreciation or encouragement would have meant a lot. After all, I was now over forty and had many years of service to the Mission to my credit. And perhaps there was a lingering feeling that 'colonial' service as it was then called in New Zealand did not necessarily qualify for the more sophisticated world of London. As far as I was concerned the policy seemed to be, 'Hold him back; slow him down; he has a lot to learn.'

As time went on the sense of frustration continued to increase. Walking down the platform to the ticket barrier at Victoria Station in the mornings, I noticed the big steel buffers built in to stop any runaway trains. Under the buffers were piles of loose gravel, designed to slow up an escaping train before it hit them. Multitudes of small gravel stones could be almost as effective in bringing the train to a full stop as the steel buffers themselves. These piles of slowing-up gravel represented to me the frustrations, the innumerable committee meetings, the endless consultations, the negative decisions and postponements, the hoary traditions and the vagueness. I truly tried to bow to the discipline of it, knowing in my heart that, as with the children of Israel, ' . . . you shall remember all the way which the Lord your God has led you these forty years in the wilderness that He might humble you, testing you to know what was in your heart, whether you would keep His commandments or not' (Deut. 8:2). I felt that if only I could stick it out it would come right in the end. And indeed it did.

During these years impatience was one of my besetting sins, and I must have been a trial to Clarence and the council with my restless ways and haste to get a move on. 'We must not pledge the future', was a cautionary note from our chairman. But the proving stage was longer than I had expected and it was years before my inner confidence was regained.

I sought relief from this painful situation in work, work and more work. I threw myself into it, especially in the form of speaking at meetings and visiting camps and missions and other activities involving being away from the office. Tension built up inside me, and I needed help but I had no one to whom I could turn. I asked our chairman to help us but he replied that he could do nothing as it was a matter for the council. But the council was often just as puzzled as we were.

There was no bitterness, anger or clamour but there was discomfort, discouragement and frustration, and because there were no clear lines of demarcation or authority, Clarence and I found ourselves struggling along like orphans in a storm. We tried to behave as Christian gentlemen but this was not enough. Our problems needed to be faced and brought out into the open.

A poignant incident illustrates the confusion of the relationship between us. On one occasion Howard Mowll, then Archbishop of Sydney and world president of Scripture Union, was in England. When Clarence and I met him neither of us was sure who should greet him first. I held back in deference to Clarence as my senior colleague and Clarence held back with some natural diffidence. There was an awkward pause which was eventually broken by the Archbishop himself who asked politely, 'Which of the two secretaries is going to greet me?'

Meanwhile I discovered Henri Fayol's book *General and Industrial Management* (Pitmans) and was intrigued to find the following:

> The desire to get away from the immediate necessity of dividing up authority between two colleagues, two friends, two members of one family, results at times, in dual command reigning at the top of a concern right from the outset. Exercising the same powers and having the same authority over the same men, the two colleagues end up inevitably with dual command and its consequences. Despite harsh lessons, instances of this sort are still numerous. New colleagues count on their mutual regard, common interest, and good sense to save them from every conflict, every serious disagreement and, save for rare exceptions, the illusion is short-lived. First, an awkwardness makes itself felt, then a certain irritation and, in time, if dual command exists, even hatred. Men cannot bear dual command. A judicious assignment of duties would have reduced the danger without entirely banishing it, for between two superiors on the same footing there must always be some question ill-defined. But it is riding for a fall to set up a business organisation with two superiors on equal footing without assigning duties and demarcating authority. In all human associations, in industry, commerce, army, home, state, dual command is a perpetual source of conflict.

How now Women's Lib. & roles of father & mother in home?

The aptness of these words to our problem astonished me and fitted our situation exactly except, thankfully, for the word 'hatred'. But at times the strain was very great. I came home one night and began to tell Marion about the difficulties and found myself sobbing, and I remember on one occasion when I tried to be frank with Clarence, my gentle friend broke down himself. But all through these difficult years our friendship was never broken. It was bruised but never broke down completely under the strain. Although we were so different in temperament we liked each other and I particularly remember one occasion when I was very touched by Clarence's warm-hearted nature. I

131

was about to set off on a long journey and Clarence, in his thoughtful way, sent me a card which read:

CHRIST
His love attend thee
His strength defend thee,
His peace commend thee
His Spirit send thee.
                                        R. E. Cleeve

We remained friends to the last and after Clarence's retirement I wrote to him after each council meeting. I also visited him during his last illness and he and his wife Dorothy always received me lovingly.

While this was going on in the background the policy was 'not in front of the children'. Quite rightly, I feel. If our differences had become a public quarrel much damage could have resulted. We found it hard to understand why it worked out as unhappily as it did, although there was sunshine as well as cloud. I suppose we were inclined to blame one another and to blame ourselves guiltily for our own all too obvious failures. Some senior members of staff, reading between the lines, took it philosophically while others exploded in hastily worded memos and had to be calmed down and have their genuine grievances dealt with. Others concentrated on their own departmental jobs and kept their heads down. We prayed together but perhaps a little too guardedly.

I kept hoping that the council would one day ask the all-important question: 'How is the joint secretaryship working?' but they did not. We can bear and endure difficulties, disappointments and struggles in the preaching of the Gospel among the children of this and other lands, but to be working at cross purposes right at the very heart and core of the Mission we had been chosen to serve, was the hardest cross to bear and we both felt it keenly.

11 'THE DEVIL IS AFTER YOU'

During the busy three months in Australia and the equally busy ones before leaving New Zealand I was conscious at times of some cardiac discomfort. While an electrocardiogram revealed that there was nothing seriously wrong with the heart the discomfort continued to be a minor nuisance, particularly in times of tension and worry. I therefore took the opportunity, on coming to London, to consult Dr. F. W. Price, a well-known heart specialist whose rooms were just round the corner from our office. After examining me he sat back in his chair and looked at me across his desk. To my astonishment his first words were, 'The devil is after you.' In my medical-student days I had made good use of this famous doctor's well-known classic, *A Textbook of the Practice of Medicine*, little thinking that I would ever meet Dr. Price personally, and still less that he would be warning me, in somewhat un-professional language about the activities of the devil. But it was not altogether surprising for I knew him to be a well-known and respected Christian.

In response to my astonished questioning about the devil being after me, he continued on a somewhat more reassuring note, saying that my heart condition was not serious but that I should change my lifestyle. 'You are a useful servant of God. The devil knows this and will do his best to bring you down if you are not more careful,' he said. I little realised at that moment how prophetic his words were to become.

He continued to warn me that I must cut down my activities, learn to delegate, be in bed by nine o'clock, take a taxi from Victoria Station to 5 Wigmore Street, follow a prescribed diet and, his final piece of advice, to apply some liniment to my chest to ease the discomfort when that became necessary. I tried to take Dr. Price's advice seriously, though my Scots instincts and early training made me draw the line at hiring taxis to and from the office at a cost of two shillings and sixpence each way, but gradually other things he had advised me to do dropped off and I carried on as before. As sometimes happens, everything seemed to go wrong at once. I was worried about my father who was lonely and ill, and in the early stages of abdominal cancer from which he later died. During his long and trying illness he prayed faithfully for his children and grandchildren and his many friends. He had been a wonderful father to us; we loved him dearly and missed him greatly. Then there was the birth of Alistair and many sleepless nights, not to mention some of the adolescent growing pains experienced by our older children and shared by us, and when these difficulties were added to the problems at the office, the accumulated burdens seemed almost intolerable.

One day in October 1948, things came to a head. I had a busy morning at the office when I found to my dismay that I had promised to speak at a lunch-hour Christian Union meeting at Sutton Boys' High School. I got away with great difficulty and dashed off to Victoria Station. I was running late and hurriedly enquired at the barrier if this was the train for Sutton. I got the impression that it was but maybe I wasn't listening carefully enough.

I sat in the carriage waiting for the train to start and tried to compose my ruffled thoughts. At last the train moved off, and after a while I began to suspect that something was wrong — we were on the way to Crystal Palace and not to Sutton. I got out and asked the guard if this was the right train. He mumbled something, waved his flag and the train began to move.

It was a wet day and I had my umbrella with me. On a sudden impulse I gave the guard a whack across the arm as he tried to prevent me from boarding the guard's van. He was furious. He stopped the train. A few heads popped out. 'You will hear more of this,' he said ominously. The station master was summoned and my name and address taken.

My apologies were disregarded and I made my miserable way home. It was now too late for Sutton and I could not face a return to the office. I was much too ashamed to tell anyone except my wife. She was equally upset and was inclined to blame herself feeling that she must have failed in some way.

One morning a pleasant young policeman called and delivered a summons for me to appear at Penge Magistrates

Court on January 7th, 1949. I was deeply upset. I realised that I needed legal advice but I was much too embarrassed and ashamed to consult my friend Derek Warren, a member of our council and a first-class lawyer, so I went to the office of Percy Holt in Purley. Mr. Holt, an elderly gentleman, pooh-poohed the whole thing saying that there was no need for me to be legally represented. 'Don't worry. You'll probably be fined ten shillings and that will be that,' he said philosophically. But I did worry and told nobody.

I appeared in the dock at Penge Magistrates Court on January 7th and was treated with courtesy, The railway authorities were represented but I can't remember a word they said. My apologies were, I think, taken into consideration and Mr. Holt proved to be right in that I was fined ten shillings with two pounds and two shillings costs. But my real worry was about the local press reporters who sat diligently taking notes.

I guessed what might happen and it did. On the following Sunday afternoon our son Graham came home saying that the boys at Crusaders had been saying that his father had been fined for striking a railway guard and that they had read about it in the local paper. I found later that there was a five-inch column right in the middle of the front page, with the headline 'Purley man's conduct earns him a fine'.

At once I telephoned Mr. W. W. Allen, our senior elder, and that evening spoke to several elders after the evening service offering my resignation from the eldership of the Assembly. Some took it lightly, some seriously and, in the event, my proffered resignation was not accepted. My colleagues at the office were kind and understanding, and so were the members of the council. The incident was not taken too seriously, but with me it went very deep. For years I could not bring myself to speak of it, and to this day I have a mental jolt whenever it crosses my mind.

One lesson at least can be drawn from all this. When we are carrying a head of emotional pressure and things are coming at us from every angle and all at once, it is important to recognise that we need help, but this is not easy, for wise and understanding father-confessors and mother-confessors are few and far between. But they are worth searching for. In these circumstances I should have done my best to find a sympathetic but objective friend to whom I could have poured out my troubles. But I was tired and dispirited and it was easier to stick it out from day to day.

This is where the local church should come in, for it should be a community of people where we can find wise and understanding helpers to whom we can turn when everything seems against us. They need not necessarily be trained counsellors, though training has great value. I had an old friend in New Zealand, quite a simple saintly old gentleman, with whom I could share my troubles and problems and with whom I could pray. He was skilled in reminding me of the promises of God and in applying the comfort of the Scriptures, well-mixed with sound advice and common sense, based on long experience. He had an impediment in his speech which meant that he did not talk overmuch and was therefore a good listener. One could implicitly rely on him to keep a confidence.

The common sense, loyalty, loving support and practical help of my wife were without price, and I confided in her at all times, but she needed one kind of help and I another. For her it was coping with our five children, including Alistair, especially during the severe 1947 winter, and my father's terminal illness, while for me it was my work at the office and with my colleagues. We helped each other all we could but we needed some outside help as well.

There is a quotation from *Macbeth* which sums it up admirably:

> Canst thou not minister to a mind diseas'd
> Pluck from the memory a rooted sorrow,
> Raze out the written troubles of the brain,
> And with some sweet oblivious antidote
> Cleanse the stuff'd bosom of that perilous stuff
> Which weighs upon the heart?

The Roman Catholic Church has something to teach us here. No doubt the practice of Confession has been abused, especially in the past but the Confessional is still in constant use in Roman Catholic churches, with trained priests available to give advice and comfort. This is not to suggest that we Protestants should make similar arrangements, but we may be all too deficient in the use of skilled pastoral care. We are not men of steel. We get hurt, do wrong, unpleasant things happen to us which are common to man, and we need help which God undoubtedly gives through the comfort of other human beings.

Protestant pastors are becoming increasingly aware of this. General medical practitioners are often used as leaning posts but it seems unfair to expect them to carry other people's emotional burdens as well as caring for their physical needs. More and more, we should be educating our churches as caring communities where there is an atmosphere of love and trust and where some who have pastoral gifts should be given specialised and formal training in these skills, developing further the gifts they already have.

As George Eliot says: 'Oh, the comfort, the inexpressible comfort of feeling safe with someone, having neither to weigh thoughts nor measure words, but pour them all out, just as they are, chaff and grain together, and a faithful hand will take and sift them, keep what is worth keeping, and with a breath of kindness blow the rest away.'

But if these experiences were hard, they also made me take stock. I realised that it was time to organise my affairs in such a way as to enable me, in my old grandmother's words, to 'keep cool, calm and collected'. I could no longer go on in this state of inner turmoil.

I began by trying to accept things just as they were but at the same time keeping my mind alert to all possible solutions.

Not long after I had appeared in the Magistrates Court I began to realise that I was more seriously in need of help than I had thought. About this time I received a letter from Mr. Keith, who urged me not to do so much. 'You are feeling the strain . . . I am so sorry to hear that you are not sleeping well. Now, do be careful and go slowly!' Kindly words and well meant, but such gentle exhortations, while appreciated, were of little use. They did not get to the root of the problem. Both Clarence and I needed leadership and action, not advice, so in January 1949, I began by drafting a memorandum to Clarence hoping to get his agreement before recommending it to the council. I suggested that the council should allow me to take over responsibility for the general administration of the

137

Mission while still continuing to recognise him as the senior partner. He did not reply to my memo, but when I discussed it with him, I found that it had caused him real distress. I did my best to comfort him, but I was much distressed myself. So the subject was dropped and we carried on as before.

Twelve months later I tried again and wrote to Mr. Keith setting out in some detail my proposals for a new adminis-trative set-up. Three weeks later a special committee was appointed to consider my proposals, in consultation with Clarence and myself. Nothing was decided, however, and things were left in abeyance for what seemed like months on end.

All I wanted from the council was a mandate and a constitutional authorisation to do certain things formally recognised as my sphere of operations. Someone said, 'Why don't you just go ahead and do it?' That was, in fact, what happened and indeed had to happen, but I did not like it and worked hard to get it regularised. The council at that time did not seem to want to give me this mandate and it was a time of heart-searching as I couldn't understand their attitude. They were all able men, successful in their own specialised spheres, but at a loss when faced with the kind of difficulties in which we were involved. The idea which they had of emergent leadership had come to a point where a firm decision was needed one way or the other. It had become too long-drawn out. Leadership is a personal skill which cannot be exercised by a corporate body. People respond to good leadership with enthusiasm and loyalty. It is hard to be loyal and enthusiastic about a committee, however excellent its individual members may be and this had proved to be the case. The advice to 'go ahead and do it' was well meant but wrong. To quote Florence Nightingale, 'Authority must not be flouted, it must be con-verted.' So early in 1950 in despair I drafted a letter to Mr. Keith to say that I was seriously considering resigning from the staff, but after sleeping on it, I decided not to send it. It was just as well for, as so often happens in a 'guided' life, help was at hand.

It was suggested that one council member be appointed to supervise the work of the two secretaries; Mr. Montague Goodman was asked to undertake this task, but declined. The council then set up a new sub-committee, consisting of two of its members, Mr. F. D. Bacon and Mr. W. G. Norris and from that moment on, things began to improve. Walter Norris was a business man with long administrative experience. He had been a managing director for many years and so fully understood the concept of management. But above all, he was able to grasp the situation.

By May, agreement was reached between Frank Bacon and Walter Norris on the one hand and Clarence and me on the other. In a letter signed by both they wrote, 'We must say how extremely appreciative we are of the spirit in which you have both listened to our suggestions and we are very thankful to God for the evident desire that everything should be done for the good of this great work in which we are all privileged to have a part.'

Attached to their letter was a brief outline of our several responsibilities, clearly defined and agreed to. A meeting had been arranged for June 6th for Clarence and myself to meet Frank Bacon and Walter Norris, but Frank did not attend and we had Walter Norris to ourselves. He answered our questions, made a number of minor decisions and told us to get on with our respective jobs and, if we had any problems, to go to him.

It was about this time that Mr. Keith told the council that, as he now lived in retirement at Milford on Sea, some ninety miles from London, he did not wish to travel to town during the following winter months and he had, therefore, decided to resign as chairman. The council urged him to continue, and after some hesitation he agreed to do so, but as he did not expect to attend the meetings regularly, the council appointed Walter Norris as deputy-chairman as from July 1950. It was emphasised that this title would not mean in any way that the holder of it would automatically succeed to the chairmanship. Mr. Norris kindly agreed, after much hesitation, to undertake this responsibility but it is rather ironic that even at council level there now appeared to be a joint sharing of the chairmanship, and lack of confidence in entrusting one individual with responsibility.

In the following year Mr. Keith eventually resigned as chairman. When the question as to who was to succeed him came up, Mr. Keith said to me, 'You have no say in this matter.' However, it was essential that the views of the secretaries should be taken into account and, in the event, we were consulted. Clarence's preference was different from mine, and I suggested that he, as the senior secretary, should have first choice, but when the chairmanship was offered to his nominee it was declined. My preference was for Walter Norris and although he was a comparative newcomer having joined the council in August 1947 and without CSSM background, he was appointed chairman in July 1951.

It may be thought that I have been unduly critical of A. B. Keith. I did not feel any criticism towards him as a person. He was a thoroughly good man, both kindly and considerate, but I do feel that he was incorrectly cast in the role as chairman.

When Walter Norris became chairman of the council in July 1951, it seemed as if new life was surging through the Movement. He had come up the hard way in business and had learned his lessons in management by practical experience. He was correctly cast as chairman. The success of any arrangement depends, not only on the qualities of the man himself, however excellent, but on his being correctly cast in the role where he can exercise his natural gifts effectively. The square peg in the round hole results only in discomfort and confusion.

Our new chairman did not interfere with the day-to-day running of the Mission, but he was available for advice and consultation when asked. He was a born leader and built us into a team. He had the skills to lead a debate and guide his council members to a firm decision. At times of crisis his tough realism and active involvement, sometimes at much emotional cost to himself, together with his instinctive understanding of the principles of human administration, cleared the air and brought peace and harmony out of muddle and confusion.

His office was just round the corner and he assured us that we could call on him at any time. I took advantage of his offer and quite often went to see him with some burden or problem. He was both firm and kind. He seemed to know by instinct that good administration included ministration as he ministered to my troubled spirit. In the years that followed I found myself exercising a similar pastoral role in relation to my colleagues.

Some months after Mr. Norris's appointment, Mr. Montague Goodman magnanimously said at a council meeting that, in his opinion, he was the best chairman that the Mission had ever had. In my heart of hearts I could not but agree. Here at last was someone who was willing to let the buck stop at him. He had the authority of his office as chairman to authenticate and encourage him and he did not hesitate to use it. He took as his motto 'To do justly and to love mercy, and to walk humbly with thy God' (Micah 6:8). And these three he faithfully exemplified, sometimes with slightly more emphasis on the justice than the mercy! But always with a true inward humility of heart and only very occasionally with a slight loss of nerve. His highest praise, used sparingly, was 'You acted correctly'. For me, at any rate, these three words have acted as a clear shaft of light in murky situations. I have owed many men and women deep debts of gratitude at various phases of my life but to none more than to Walter Norris. This was not, however, because he favoured me rather than Clarence. In fact, no one could have been more scrupulously fair. Indeed, I felt, and was happy to feel, that at times he favoured Clarence and was tough with me. I liked it that way. I would rather have tough treatment than the awful feeling that I was the chairman's favourite.

In the autumn of 1952 Clarence said that he would retire when he reached the age of sixty-five, which was unusual in those days. But again the council were in no hurry to commit themselves as I explained in a letter to my wife:

Mr. Norris saw Clarence and me and explained that the council were very reluctant to contemplate losing Clarence in three years' time, but that, as the suggestion had come from him (and that, said W.G.N. [Walter Norris], was a great gesture on Clarence's part), they were prepared to accept it. With reference to myself, they recognised the need to plan ahead and for that reason they were prepared to say that, barring any unforeseen and unexpected major happenings, I would become general secretary on Clarence's retirement. I found it difficult to accept that they could not specifically make a definite promise, but it was to be understood to be sufficiently definite to enable us to plan with that

141

in mind, the planning to be done by W.G.N., C.H.M.F. [Clarence Foster] and myself, but with the thought that it would, in all probability, be me who would have to put the plan into effect. W.G.N. was most emphatic that no hint of this must be allowed to leak out.

I have not had time to sort out my thinking about this but I had a very good straightforward talk with W.G.N. afterwards and am prepared to accept his leadership. I feel that there is an understanding between him and me which, after all, is the most important thing, and I feel sure that it will work out all right and that the dreadful old difficulties of the joint secretaryship are now over. They largely arose, I think, from vague leadership at the top and that chapter was closed when W.G.N. took the chair.

But, although I accepted these facts and appeared outwardly to have been philosophical about them, I was really very hurt that somehow I still did not seem to have earned the whole-hearted support and confidence of the council and that despite my hard work and love for the Mission, I still hadn't quite 'made the grade'. If only the council could have added a few words of appreciation and encouragement it would have made all the difference.

As things worked out I was now free to press ahead with various plans and projects and this I did feeling, at last, that I had a sufficient mandate from the council to do so.

These difficult years were a time of spiritual growth and development probably more than at any time in my life. Lessons were learned in the school of discipline and prayer as never before or since.

Although I couldn't see it at the time, good did come out of all this muddle. Indeed, someone said to me years later that it was during these years of background difficulty that the work grew and prospered at home and abroad. One well-known Christian leader went so far as to say that it was during this time that the Scripture Union was brought into the 20th century.

Following this period of difficulty and stress Mr. Norris wrote to me in February 1952:

142

Whatever task God has for you in the future I am convinced that you need to be trained for it in more ways than one. Honours degrees are only obtainable by harder work and more (and perhaps disagreeable) self-discipline than ordinary passes. Perhaps you are in God's honours school. Success, I suggest, will come not by merely putting up with distasteful circumstances but by taking a positive line in regard to them, and being triumphant in the real sense of the word.

A certain kind of maturity, uncommon and extremely valuable, is developed only by these kind of experiences and perhaps you have been selected for the training because of a high task that lies ahead in God's purposes . . . I hope that you will take this letter as another proof of my warm love in Christ and of my deep interest in your welfare and work, particularly in regard to our joint responsibilities and labours.

This is the main part of my reply to Walter Norris's letter:

It is quite true, as you say, that we cannot expect one hundred per cent unity throughout the Mission where there is disunity at the top. But that disunity at the top is organisational as well as personal. Clarence and I began as friends who recognised that joint leadership was very often unsuccessful. But we counted on our mutual regard, common trust, good sense and prayers to save us from conflict and disagreement. Gradually however, the effects of a dual control became evident, strive against it though we did. In May 1951, after five difficult years, the work was divided between us. This brought some personal relief but it has not as yet promoted unity at headquarters. Even if we had been naturally suited to each other it would have been difficult, but there are wide disparities of age, temperament, training and cast of mind. These differences, however much we try to over-come them, communicate themselves imperceptibly to our principal colleagues and affect morale. The longer this continues the more difficult it becomes to correct it.

I do not wish to labour this point, but to face it frankly, as one of the main difficulties. Having done so, I can only say that I am willing and ready to make a fresh start under your leadership and along the lines proposed in your letter. The real reply must be in actions . . . rather than words.

In later years Walter Norris and I became close friends and worked happily together, but that was when I was general secretary and he was chairman and a working friendship in these circumstances was quite in order.

In any organisation where the chairman and general secretary or chief executive officer work harmoniously together, they form the axis round which the whole enterprise revolves. One represents the council and the other the staff, and when a good relationship is established between them an example is set and its influence percolates throughout the whole organisation, resulting in an efficient and happy team.

One of the lessons to be learned from these difficulties was that whatever may have been our personal faults and failures, and there certainly were some, a very large part of our problem was the failure to recognise the importance of correct structure into which the various personalities could fit.

12   RELUCTANT ADMINISTRATOR

During the war-years in New Zealand it became increasingly difficult to fulfil the multiple roles of a schools' travelling secretary, a general preacher and Bible teacher and children's evangelist, together with overall administration. What had begun as a simple, straightforward enterprise had grown into a movement and an organisation calling for administrative supervision, and it gradually became apparent that the latter would have to be my role. Younger men and women were more suitable for the field work. They could leave their teaching or ministry in a local church and give a few of their best years to an evangelistic, inspirational and Bible teaching ministry, and then return to their calling enriched by this wider experience. But someone was needed to provide continuity and to ensure that the organisation was running smoothly.

The decision to give myself mainly to administrative activities was not an easy one. I kicked against it, and in the early stages tried to fulfil several different roles at once, nearly cracking up in the process, but I gradually came to the place of willingness to do what the law of the situation demanded — plain duty.

It was certainly an honourable vocation, for administration is one of the gifts of the Spirit referred to in 1 Corinthians 12:28.

We may define an administrator as a person who organises and manages the affairs of others in an orderly way, assisting them in the fulfilment of an agreed objective. Although I did not recognise it at the time my acceptance of this role was to prepare the way for a similar but more demanding job later.

In the New Zealand days there was a steady stream of mainly young people coming to Christ month by month through our ministry, especially in the schools, camps and seaside missions, but when I came to London I knew of very few, very few indeed, who were converted to Christ as a result of my direct and personal effort. My time, together with my senior colleagues and office staff, became fully occupied with providing back-up services for a great company of evangelists,

145

schools' travelling secretaries and editors, and thousands of camp officers and beach mission workers whose influence extended across the country and worldwide. My job was to see that there was the necessary prayer support and moral and financial support, and to ensure that well-designed, unobtrusive, congenial, prayerful, well-oiled administration in an atmosphere of encouragement provided good working conditions for the front-line evangelists. But the administrative burden in England was much greater and more complex than in New Zealand where we had an office of six, and less than that number in the field. In these circumstances I found myself floundering with an inadequate knowledge of business methods for which a medical training had not prepared me.

Looking back I now realise that my first introduction to ideas about business administration came when I was a young man listening to the conversations of my uncle Nigel Laird. As I have mentioned earlier, my grandfather John Laird, had started a stationery business, but he was a friendly, convivial and rather impulsive man, not endowed with much in the way of business instincts. With a growing family of six boys and one girl and a shaky business something had to be done, so Nigel left Greenock Academy when he was still in his early teens and went into business with his father. He showed considerable acumen, and business gradually improved, but relationships between young Nigel and his easy-going father became increasingly strained. Eventually in desperation Nigel turned for advice to my grandmother's brother, Robert Barr, who had made a fortune in the then flourishing Scottish industries of distilling and shipbuilding. Great-uncle Robert, with shrewd insight into the potential abilities of the youthful Nigel, advised him to form a company in which Nigel would be the chief executive, while his father would be somewhat of a figure-head with a roving commission to make business contacts and cultivate the goodwill of customers. A legal agreement was drawn up in which Nigel and his father bound themselves to certain clearly defined roles and responsibilities. In telling me about this my uncle's jaw set as he said with great intensity: 'and I made sure that the agreement was gas tight'. From then on muddle and confusion were replaced by a well-organised business which prospered greatly.

While still in New Zealand in 1940 I read Seebohm Rowntree's book, *The Human Factor in Business*. He was one of many outstanding Quaker industrialists whose record of applying Christian principles to business was perhaps unequalled in his time. He laid down as a first principle that authority depends on justice. Great care was taken to ensure that there was fair play at all levels and all management decisions were subject to an appeal committee. As long ago as 1921 the management proposed the appointment of a trained psychologist to select employees for different kinds of work. This aroused much suspicion and opposition, but eventually resulted in misfits being reduced from twenty per cent to five per cent. He stressed that rough justice was not good enough, on the principle that if justice is to be done at all, it must be done in minute particulars. These and many other reforms were well before their time. As a result of good working conditions, holidays with pay, good wages, profit sharing, democratic principles, personnel management, medical care, tact, a co-operative spirit and, above all, justice and good leadership, good workers were attracted and retained. Rowntree claimed that these results showed that communism could not give the workers a better deal than this way of handling a capitalistic organisation.

In April 1943, J. H. Oldham's Christian Newsletter contained a review of a book by James Burnham, *The Managerial Revolution*, in which he described the emergence of a class of managers in industry having interests and objects separate and distinct from those of capital and labour. Burnham forecast that the function of management or administration had become more important because of the rapid rate of change in our modern society, and also because of the emergence in big business of larger units in industry. He urged the importance of administration as a professional skill and claimed that training for administrative leadership would grow men, in the sense that the processes of production should develop the qualities of the producers, in contrast to the depersonalisation of men and women in industry or unemployment. John Ruskin has a phrase for it, 'In our factories we fabricate everything except men.'

In the autumn of 1947 we were invited to spend an evening

with friends to enjoy some music. Before leaving and while waiting for my wife to put on her coat I glanced at my friend's books. A slim volume entitled *Elements of Administration* by L. Urwick (Pitmans) caught my eye. I asked if I might borrow it, and on returning home began to read. The first few pages introduced me to a way of thinking about administrative problems which was new and exciting, and by the time I had read the whole book I was convinced that I had at least the beginnings of a solution to the administrative muddles at Wigmore Street. As I now realise the discovery of this book was indeed no mere chance. Here were possibilities for acquiring the understanding I so obviously needed. Books were the answer!

Urwick claimed that in the complex world of western civilisation, individual opportunism was destructive of orderly, secure co-operative living. He argued that the only way to deal with muddle and confusion was to begin by drawing up a plan setting out the ideal structure, and then to fit the personalities into the structure. He maintained that it was a mistake to begin with the personalities and then try to make the structure fit in with them, or to try to do without structure altogether and just go forward into the future one step at a time, thus gradually drifting into an unworkable organisation. Not that the plan should be rigid and unchangeable. Modifications could often be made, so long as there was a plan or working model as a guide and a structure in which individuals would find their place and setting.

He emphasised that the recognition of the need for an ordered structure is of great importance because it can make or mar peoples' lives. The Romans in their love of order had a word for all this. It is in the form of a Latin rhyming couplet which can be translated:

> No high quality avails
> Where the rule of order fails.

There are some people who find it difficult to work in a structured situation, while for others it is essential for their emotional well-being. Many of our schools' travelling secretaries come from the structured community of school life into the less structured job of a travelling secretary. Where

148

their work is planned and supervised all is well, but for certain people in certain situations, lack of structure can be disastrous. In one of the developing countries, an English girl teaching in a well organised school, joined the staff of Scripture Union as a schools' travelling secretary. She had a family history of nervous stress and this had been underestimated in giving her what proved to be an overdemanding assignment. Very little was done to guide and supervise her, and not knowing how to proceed she found herself more and more embarrassed and confused. By temperament she was dependent on the ordered life of a well-run school, and the sudden transition from a structured to an unstructured situation resulted in severe mental and emotional stress. She came home to England, and was given hospitality in a Christian home, but was later admitted to hospital where she died from an overdose of drugs.

People need adequate supervising; they need leadership, they need pastoral care, and it seems that these essentials were lacking for this young woman.

Urwick's argument which hit me with tremendous force went on to say that lack of design is illogical, cruel, wasteful and inefficient.

It is illogical because design must come first, as with an architect, or an engineer or town planner. It is unreasonable to expect any individual to be appointed to an important position without a clear idea of the part which that position is meant to play in the general pattern of which it is a component. But it is also cruel, because the main sufferers from a lack of design are the individuals who work in the undertaking. If an employer appoints a man without any clear idea in his own mind of the exact duties for which he requires him, and the kind of qualifications needed to discharge these duties, the chances are that he will blame the man if the results do not correspond with his vague notion of what he is wanted for.

Also it is wasteful, because if there is no structure every change in personnel through retirement, promotion or leaving, becomes a crisis and an experiment in personalities.

To quote him directly on lack of design, Urwick adds:

It is inefficient, because if an organisation is not founded upon principles, then those directing it have nothing to fall

149

back on but personalities. The personal touch is important. Kindliness, tact, generosity of spirit as between colleagues are invaluable lubricants in any kind of undertaking; from superior to subordinate they are an obvious duty. But the administrator who tries to substitute amiability for definite planning in questions of organisation will find sooner rather than later that the 'personal touch' issues in an epidemic of touchiness. Unless there are principles on which he can fall back and which are understood by everyone in the undertaking, it is inevitable that in matters of promotion and similar issues men will start 'playing politics'.

Emphasis has been laid on this question of thinking consciously and technically about organisation, of laying out structure first and not thinking about individuals till structure has been determined, because it is still rare to find any general acceptance of this principle. The majority of social groups being left to grow like Topsy find, sooner rather than later, that Topsy has married Turvy.

In short, a very large proportion of the friction and confusion in current society, with its manifest consequences in human suffering may be traced directly to faulty organisation in the structural sense.

I soon discovered other books dealing with administration and eventually collected quite a shelf-full. I tried to find a centre where it would be possible to get some further training and consulted Frederick Catherwood. He told me that there was little to be found in England at that time, and that he himself went to America from time to time to get up-to-date with the latest thinking on the subject.

I found it hard to assume the servant role, for that is what administration is all about. After all, administration is but another word for ministration, and ministration is another word for service.

Under modern conditions the practice of good administration as an art and a science should be a recognised skill to professional standards, calling for training, study and specialised expertise. I found that some of my colleagues did not share this thinking, and regarded my time spent in studying business books as somewhat unspiritual. My reply was, and still is, that no one suggests that it is unspiritual for Christian men or women to train as accountants, lawyers, architects or doctors, and to use these skills in God's service, so why not as professional administrators?

But my critics deserved a more satisfying answer, and this I found, not in modern business books, though they are useful in their proper place, but in one of the greatest themes recurring throughout Scripture; namely that 'Order is God's first law'. While it is true that God is love, He is also a God of order, and where good order prevails there is a strong and orderly framework in which love can flourish best. Order and love are not mutually exclusive but are complementary to each other.

The first chapter of Genesis presents us with a majestic panorama in which the heavens and the earth are seen as being 'without form and void with darkness over the face of the abyss' (Gen. 1:2, N.E.B.). This is followed by an orderly development in the work of creation, culminating in the declaration that 'God saw everything that He had made, and behold it was very good.'

Then comes the picture of a garden and the love of a man and a woman, a scene of beauty and order, yet tragically destroyed by man's wilful disobedience.

The book of Exodus describes the escape from Egypt of the Children of Israel including an unruly 'mixed multitude'. At Mount Sinai Moses is given the 'pattern in the Mount' and under his leadership the encampment is laid out with areas allotted to each tribe with the Tabernacle at the centre, itself a place of beauty and order.

The most tragic book in the Old Testament is the book of Judges, descriptive of a period when law and order had broken down because there was no king in Israel and every man did that which was right in his own eyes.

In the New Testament, and especially in the Gospels, there are recurrent references to the Kingdom of God, the Kingdom of order, justice, peace and love. Similarly the apostle Paul refers to the church in Ephesus as a 'harmonious *structure* knit together by the joints with which it is provided, [and which] grows by the proper functioning of individual parts to its full maturity in *love*' (Eph. 4:16, Phillips).

151

The New Testament finally ends with a sublime vision of the heavenly city glowing with beauty and order. At last the 'kingdom of the world has become the kingdom of our Lord and His Christ, and He shall reign for ever and ever' (Rev. 11:15).

Man's besetting sin throughout history including the present time has been to reverse the process by bringing chaos out of cosmos. Yet God will triumph in the end.

An old puritan writer says of the Trinity that 'God Himself is a sweet society', and John Greenleaf Whitier has a word for us all:

> Drop Thy still dews of quietness
> Till all our strivings cease:
> Take from our souls the strain and stress,
> And let our ordered lives confess
> The beauty of Thy peace.

13 SCRIPTURE UNION FLOURISHES

The next sixteen years were full of interest and encouragement, and under Walter Norris's wise and firm chairmanship the council prospered. The inevitable problems cropped up but we were now in a position to deal with them. Some of those who joined us had served with distinction during the war and had greatly matured as a result of their experiences of working in the framework of the services' administrative structures. At our staff meetings our council room became crowded as we met every Tuesday in the lunch hour for prayer and discussion, when we brought one another up-to-date with the latest news and developments, each taking an interest in the affairs of the others. This resulted in a stimulating cross-fertilisation of ideas, and it also meant that we were able to discuss various proposals which could then be considered by the council.

Council members were welcome to attend these meetings but did not do so, tactfully leaving us to our own devices, but they were helpfully involved with the departmental heads in a series of sub-committees.

Each week I had lunch with the chairman, and by the time our suggestions had been discussed with him they were ready to be put up to the council, in the form of written recommendations. These the council considered, very often making helpful modifications, and they then, in most cases, gave the go-ahead for action.

As time went on some of our colleagues left us and went on to other appointments in Christian publishing, in the teaching profession and one in the B.B.C. We did nothing to hold them back for we felt that this was our contribution to the welfare of the Kingdom of God as a whole. We had provided them with an informal training school and they were, in a sense, our graduates. The Scripture Union Movement did not suffer, for men and women of similar calibre to those we had lost remained with us, while there has never been a lack of younger men and women coming on.

In the country generally we saw signs of growth. There were approximately 350,000 Scripture Union members and 9,000 SU secretaries, and about sixty camps and forty seaside missions. The Caravan Mission to Village Children was at work in twenty-seven English counties, and there were new developments in hundreds of schools organised by the Inter-School Christian Fellowship. The Sunday School department flourished under the leadership of Reginald Hill and there was a growing publishing programme and far-reaching developments overseas.

During these years I continued to apply administrative principles to our detailed and complex organisation by modifying and adapting them to the different motivation and atmosphere of a Christian organisation such as ours, and while keeping this in mind I urged the need to bring in an outside consultant. Somewhat hesitantly the council agreed, but stipulated that his investigations and report should cover only the accounts and business side of our activities. Charles Henshall who had succeeded Hubert Smith as our business manager in 1957 found the exercise traumatic. The recommendations of the consultant were not entirely acceptable, although some were of value, but the main benefit was that it taught us to think in new administrative categories and to use modern equipment essential to our survival in the late twentieth century. As the years went by we made use of other consultants at all levels in our organisation and we also arranged for some of our colleagues to go on special courses in business administration, all with undoubted benefit.

Pastoral care for my more immediate colleagues became important, and there were opportunities for inspirational ministry at conferences, training weekends and preaching at church services, but most of my time had to be given to the overall administration of the Mission's affairs, so much so, that one of my colleagues remarked, 'We don't want our leader to be lost behind a paper curtain.' Among these responsibilities was that of ensuring that our financial resources were reasonably adequate for our staff members and their families. It was not always easy for well-off council members to realise the struggles of some of the staff members to keep their heads above the worry level financially. On one occasion when the salaries of some evangelists were being considered, one member of the committee who apparently thought that the proposed increases were too generous exclaimed, 'But, Mr. Chairman, where is the element of sacrifice?' Where indeed? But that incident happened many years ago. In recent decades our council has consistently striven to 'do justice and love mercy' in providing realistic financial support for the staff.

In 1953 we were suffering from a shortage of office accommodation and this put an added strain on some of our colleagues who had to squeeze up and share offices. We were at a loss to know what to do and prayed much about this at our weekly staff meetings.

One day, during the lunch hour, I went for a breather, taking a walk round the surrounding streets. On the way back to the office I walked down Marylebone Lane and saw a 'For Sale' notice. It was number forty-seven. Without more ado, I called at the estate agent's office and found that the asking price was £35,000. On surveying the interior, first impressions were rather unfavourable. It appeared to be structurally sound, but at first sight unsuitable for office accommodation.

The next six months were a period of painful indecision. Both the council and myself, being unused to property deals of this magnitude, were hesitant and doubtful. Some who had not inspected the building expressed quite strong views. When I described the location of Marylebone Lane, and mentioned the fact that there were a couple of pubs nearby, Mr. Goodman thought that it would not be a suitable place for our CSSM ladies to go to. The subject was discussed at one monthly council meeting after another. The council changed its mind more than once and it was finally decided to take no action.

At this juncture we had to let matters rest as I had been invited to go on a world tour including Australia and New Zealand and had to be away from the office for nearly six months.

On my return, I found that the pressure on the office space at Wigmore Street was even more acute and that irritation and discontent were in the air. Then, to my great surprise, I found that the Marylebone Lane property was once again on the market but speculators had bought it and the asking price was

155

now £45,000. I for one was fully convinced that this was the Lord's provision for us, and although the council were still hesitant, they eventually agreed. An appeal was made to our supporters and the response was such in gifts and loans that we were able to go ahead. The largest single loan, from a husband and wife, amounted to £10,000. £20,000 was spent on turning the factory-type building into offices, and on March 15th, 1956, the building was opened and dedicated by Walter Norris. To my great chagrin, I was confined to bed with an acute attack of mumps and was unable to be present.

In the event, our new offices gave us much satisfaction, and we were able to let the upper floors of the building in Wigmore Street, retaining the ground-floor shop.

I have long been convinced that the best investment for a charitable body is the possession of freehold offices, even if at first the building has to be heavily mortgaged. If this was so in those days it is certainly much more so in the current days of inflation.

The move to Marylebone Lane had brought relief from pressure on the office accommodation. But there was another form of pressure which called for attention arising from the growth of our movement worldwide.

It had fallen to my lot to be mainly responsible for what was then known as the 'overseas' side of our work. This was an aspect of my job which I greatly enjoyed. Every year, with a few exceptions, I responded to invitations or took the initiative to visit and to try to help our colleagues in Europe, North America, Australia, New Zealand and some smaller centres. It was a constantly stimulating experience to make new friends, to visit new countries, to learn from the experience of others. In this way an invisible but strong web of friendship and goodwill came to be built up around the world.

Inevitably the growth of our movement in many different countries increased the flow of correspondence and administrative work. Once again, the administration became over-taxed, for London was still the world headquarters. It became increasingly impossible for the small administrative staff in London to cope with this worldwide movement. There was a danger, as someone had put it, of apoplexy at the centre and stagnation at the circumference.

Out of these experiences the idea grew that the time had come to arrange for the leaders of our worldwide fellowship to come together and put into some ordered constitutional form the movement which had hitherto been loosely linked across the world.

With invaluable help from my legally-trained colleague, Michael Hews, a series of memoranda covering all aspects of our work were prepared and circulated in advance, allowing time for considered replies to be returned. These were then incorporated into fresh drafts which, in turn, were sent out to delegates. By the time the conference met, much of the spade-work had been done. The ground to be covered, however, was very extensive; the making of constitutions and the defining of policies on a wide range of subjects are time-consuming tasks.

The conference assembled in May 1960 at the Quaker conference centre at Old Jordans in Buckinghamshire, where William Penn is buried. The delegates consisted, for the most part, of the chairman and general secretary of the main self-governing councils representing Australia, New Zealand, South Africa, Switzerland, England, Scotland, France, North America, India and Japan. They were an outstanding body of men and one woman — Claire-Lise de Benoit, representing French-speaking Switzerland.

Derek Warren had succeeded Walter Norris as chairman of the council in November 1959. He proved to be an excellent chairman of the conference with his trained legal mind and a keen interest in international affairs, and he was ably assisted by Alan Kerr of Australia and Armin Hoppler of Switzerland as the two deputy-chairmen.

The conference proved to be a watershed in the history of our movement. From then on, London was no longer the world headquarters. I was asked to undertake the task of being secretary to the newly formed international council but I did not feel that I could combine this with the general secretaryship of the work in Britain, so Armin Hoppler was invited to accept this important appointment, and to everyone's pleasure he agreed to do so. This meant that the international office would now be located in Switzerland and the British movement would take its place as one of the

157

self-governing independent councils, but as it was the founding member it was still regarded as the parent body.

The new international office was very modest consisting of Armin Hoppler on a part-time basis assisted by Elizabeth Müller. This arrangement was kept deliberately low-key and at the time of writing is still limited to two — Nigel Sylvester and Jenny Brewster. Thus a centralised bureaucracy is avoided and responsibility is delegated to the regional offices.

The first task of the international council was to review the worldwide scene and settle priorities, to adopt a doctrinal statement and to consider aims, methods and basic philosophy. It also drew up a constitution, skilfully framed by two experienced lawyers — Otto Dose of South Africa, and Derek Warren assisted by Michael Hews.

Geographical areas of responsibility were defined and the name of the Movement was changed from the Children's Special Service Mission to Scripture Union. Paragraphs were agreed defining relationships with the Churches, with the IVF (now the UCCF) and other evangelical youth movements. Decisions were made about the copyright of Scripture Union publications, the choice of SU daily readings, our literature programme, bookshops, schools work, children's evangelism, principles of financial support and plans for the centenary, which would fall due in 1967.

By this bold, imaginative decentralisation the London office was relieved of a heavy burden of responsibility. It was realised that one of the most important results of the conference was the formation of friendships between the leaders from all over the world. It was found that Christian love and fellowship in conjunction with constitutional arrangements, proved the best of all cements. At Old Jordans the bonds of friendship and mutual confidence and goodwill were drawn closer. Spiritual values were created, and there was true unity without one dissenting voice.

I had the responsibility of conducting morning worship, and we studied together the current Scripture Union readings which were in the prophecy of Jeremiah. We were all deeply conscious of the appositeness of the words of this great prophet. In some small measure we shared his burning zeal for the word of the Lord as in the words of chapter 20:9. 'Then his word was imprisoned in my body, like a fire blazing in my heart and I was weary with holding it under' (NEB). Our task was not to hold it under but to let it out and to spread the prophetic word across the world.

The Old Jordans' conference was not only a watershed in the history of our movement, for it might be more appropriate to describe it as a new birth. Nicodemus's question, 'Can a man be born when he is old?' could apply not to individuals only but to the rebirth of a corporate body, as in Ezekiel's vision of the hoped-for rebirth of Israel from its dry and scattered bones (Ezek. 37:1–14). When the need for such a rebirth is recognised, the likelihood of a somewhat painful birth struggle must be faced and accepted. The new life may be strangled at birth or may be welcomed and given recognition and encouragement. Individuals must be willing for personal self-sacrifice for the good of the whole. The question must be answered: 'What is best for the glory of God and for the boys and girls and men and women we serve?' The question as to what is best for the good of the organisation and its leaders and members must take second place. Old societies like old men can easily become set in their ways, stiff in their movements and with vision and insight dimmed by reason of age. I feel sure that at Old Jordans, as in Australia in 1944, we shared in just such a rebirth, but the new growth could not be hurried. There are times when, like the Apostle Paul, we have to travail in birth, individually or corporately, until Christ be formed in us. Every human organisation has within it the seeds of its own decay. It must, therefore, re-examine itself or be re-examined from outside from time to time. If it is to survive it must be reborn. The sixteenth-century reformers understood this when they took as one of their mottoes for the Church the words *Semper Reformanda* — always needing to be reformed.

If something like this fails to happen, the whole corporate body becomes imperceptibly stiff, sclerosed, complacent and lifeless. Without realising what is happening, the original freshness and inspiration can die and the organisation can become something quite different or even opposed to the original vision. Centralised bureaucracies can turn inwards and feed upon themselves and fail to fulfil the reason for their

159

creation. If an attitude of laissez-faire takes over, we could one day find that changes have taken place, but they will be changes of decay instead of renewal. Renewal and revival are for new *life*, reformation is for new and better *order*. Both are needed. Only by deliberate conscious effort, by spiritual self-examination, renewal and change can we do God's work in the world today in any effective sense.

The Old Jordans' conference spent much time in drawing up a constitutional framework within which the spiritual life of the movement could find its ordered development, and through which it could flow smoothly and without frustration and friction. Many a fine work for God has been ruined because zeal outran wisdom and there was enthusiasm without order, leading to muddle, frustration and division. Equally, there have been movements where the organisation has been exalted and spiritual life has been starved. Organisation is a good servant and in the modern world we cannot exist without it, but it is just as certainly a bad master. We must see that the 'servant' does a good job, but that he knows his place and keeps to it in subordination to higher values. When Moses met God on the mount he was given two things, a vision and a pattern. If we have vision but no plan we shall merely be useless visionaries. If we have a plan neatly cut and dried, without a vision we could become unimaginative bureaucrats. We need both and we need them in due balance and proportion.

Just as at Old Jordans we had embarked on a policy of decentralisation internationally, so we came to believe that a policy of decentralisation nationally would benefit areas outside London. Having lived in Glasgow, not London, and Wellington, not Auckland, I knew well the feeling of those who live outside the main cities where too much attention is devoted to the centre. If we formed committees and located staff strategically in the country with control of their own affairs, might there not be a flowering of SU activity? This is exactly what happened. Scotland and the North of Ireland had long had their own advisory committees. Now these were given independent council status within a regional framework. Then the London council set up regional headquarters in Manchester, Norfolk and Bristol with staff assigned to develop

SU as fully as possible in their areas. It worked well, and yet was also the cause of much heart-searching and difficulty when it became advisable to transfer some loyalties to their area councils from London.

The Caravan Mission too became integrated with the work as a whole, and there are still children's evangelists working in various areas of the country, though conditions no longer require the use of a caravan.

14 WORLDWIDE GROWTH

It would be impossible to include a detailed account of the various travels undertaken during my twenty-five years in London. Of the many interesting experiences I have selected mainly those which led to further important developments.

In early April 1946, I was in Oxford attending the IVF committee for international relationships. Having a cup of tea in a café, I noticed that a young lady sitting nearby was wearing a Scripture Union badge. Speaking impeccable English she told me that her name was Claire-Lise de Benoit, and that she was from Switzerland. She had called at 5 Wigmore Street a few days earlier and had met Mr. Hubbard. I already knew that Mr. Hubbard did not look with favour on the rather independent Scripture Union developments in Switzerland and consequently his interview with Miss de Benoit had been somewhat formal. She had then proceeded to Oxford and thus our 'chance' meeting came about.

Claire-Lise told me a thrilling story of Scripture Union developments in Switzerland under the inspired leadership of Ernst Aebi and invited me to visit Switzerland and see for myself. I needed no second invitation and with the council's approval I set off. My love of trains was stimulated by the excitement of travelling on the famous Orient Express from Paris, stopping at Lausanne on its way to Istanbul. We travelled through devastated areas on our way through France and early next morning arrived at Vallorbe on the Swiss frontier. It will always remain in my memory, that calm early morning beauty of the lovely Swiss countryside with its green fields, picturesque chalets and, later, the blue waters of Lac Léman. There to meet me at Lausanne station were Claire-Lise and Ernst Aebi.

Switzerland on that sunny June morning seemed like a glimpse of heaven. Britain, France and Germany were deeply scarred under the ugly wounds of war, deprivation and suffering, but here was a haven of peace, plenty, security, unspoiled beauty, and best of all warm Christian love and friendship. Sitting in the sunshine enjoying strawberries and cream and looking out over the shining lake to the French mountains beyond, I was like a man in a dream.

My new friends unfolded a story of Scripture Union development in Switzerland which astonished me. There were over forty thousand members using Scripture Union notes, mostly in French, but with growing numbers in German. Like New Zealand, Switzerland had used the opportunity of freedom from the terror of war to build up a Christian youth movement and this it had done to great effect.

Ernst Aebi was the inspirational leader. Alert, enthusiastic, musical, warm and friendly, he had the magic touch of a great evangelist and handled crowded meetings with superb skill. Combined with his gift of evangelism Ernst had the ability of being a very good administrator which was unusual. In fact, one of his relaxations was to sit doing his accounts! In his early days he had been associated with some Pentecostal groups but had gradually moved away from that emphasis. He retained, however, the warmth and enthusiasm which had first attracted him. He was also tolerant of others who did not see things as he did, and speaking of a certain German pastor, he said: 'You see, John, he's a *very* fine man but just a leetle bit under the law.' Although he never said so, I think he found me a 'leetle bit under the law' too, for in those days I went to some length to avoid travelling on Sundays, even to the extent of postponing my return journey to England to avoid doing so.

It was the 1946 Whit Sunday weekend at the time of my visit and the annual Scripture Union youth weekend was about to take place. On the Friday evening they began to arrive, fresh-faced, healthy young men and women, the girls in brightly coloured clothes and many wearing the green and gold Scripture Union badge. The SU flag fluttered at the masthead against the beauty of the beech trees. After their morning Bible study they streamed out onto the grassy area surrounded by trees and danced simple country dances with great joy.

Saturday and Sunday were indeed great days. The general atmosphere was one of joy and happiness; many of the hymns chosen were those composed by Claire-Lise and Elsie Aebi and they were sung with great fervour. I preached for the first

163

time by interpretation and with Claire-Lise and her father, Dr. de Benoit, as skilled interpreters, I found it surprisingly easy.

As time went on, Switzerland became the key to open doors in most countries of Western Europe, first under the leadership of Ernst Aebi, who had relinquished the principalship of the Emmaus Bible School to devote himself to SU in Switzerland, and later under the wise leadership of Armin Hoppler.

In April 1948, Ernst Aebi, Armin Hoppler, then chairman of the Swiss-German Scripture Union committee, Jacob Bernhardt, who was in charge of relief work, and I set off for Germany. As we travelled one of my colleagues pointed out in the distance the place of one of the German concentration camps and we were filled with horror as we thought of the terrible atrocities, especially those directed against the Jews. It would have been easy to feel resentful and with some justification, but our present task was to deal with the situation as we found it.

As our car breasted the hills surrounding Wuppertal, we had our first terrible view of this once prosperous but now ruined city. Wuppertal had been badly bombed towards the end of the war and three years later its inhabitants were trying to eke out a miserable existence in cellars, crowded air-raid shelters and overcrowded houses. Food was desperately scarce and of poor quality. It was estimated that forty-six per cent of the population had tuberculosis resulting from overcrowding and undernourishment.

The Swiss Scripture Union had sent relief to Christian agencies in the form of tons of potatoes and a steady stream of clothing, footwear and tinned milk. Everywhere we went we found that practical help and the preaching of the Gospel went hand in hand.

Near Wuppertal we visited some local barracks where men had recently arrived having been prisoners in the Russian zone. They came in thin, haggard and utterly worn out; a few days later, as they began to eat more food, their faces, limbs and bodies became swollen with dropsy, one of the after-effects of starvation. Many had not heard of their families for years for the Russians had allowed no correspondence. A number of them refused to speak to us at all and lay wide-eyed and silent on their rough beds. To others we sought to speak of Christ and to give some practical relief. They craved cigarettes and these we gave them. Poor men! How we pitied these men who had so recently been our enemies. Among these poor wrecks of humanity was a little group of Christians, each with a precious Bible beside his bed.

Before we left Germany, Ernst, in his spontaneous way, insisted that every item of clothing or luggage which we could spare should be given away. He emptied out his suitcase on the table and, at my invitation, rifled my suitcase too for anything that could be spared. In the end he gave away the suitcase itself and said, 'John, give them your watch too. I'll give you another one when we get back to Switzerland.' I am glad to say that he forgot to do so!

On our return journey to Switzerland we noted that the British had been carrying off machinery from the German factories and the French driving the German cattle to French farms. Ironically the machinery soon became obsolete and the Germans had the advantage of building modern factories from scratch. In the years that followed, a Germany which had been bitterly humiliated, became one of the most prosperous nations of the world.

In *The Good Seed*, John Pollock refers to 1954 as the *annus mirabilis* of Scripture Union. It was the year of the Billy Graham Crusade in Harringay which resulted in an increase in the circulation of Scripture Union notes by 60,000 new readers in a single year. For me personally it included a journey of six months and 35,000 miles around the world. The main objective was to assist in developing the work of Scripture Union in all its aspects in the countries we visited, and over the next ten years I came to fulfil, in an informal way, the role of international secretary until my friend Armin Hoppler took it over officially.

The world tour of 1954 took the form of conferences with national leaders, innumerable committee meetings, policy discussions, future planning of literature and finance, visits to offices and bookshops, meetings in private homes, student groups, radio messages and, perhaps most valuable of all, countless personal conversations, often late into the night.

When invited to attend the Australian and New Zealand federal conference during this world tour I had not intended to visit Singapore, but I found that there were some flourishing Scripture Union branches and bookshops there which received supplies from London, so I arranged to break my journey for a couple of days and see how they were getting on.

What I found was beyond my expectations. Mr. Ralph Mitchell, a humble civil servant, a national of Singapore and the secretary of a large Scripture Union branch, arranged a crowded programme. He was one of many who were prepared to work for a modest but secure livelihood, thus enabling them to devote a large part of their time to the development of Christian work.

My first assignment was at the Anglo-Chinese school, and as I faced eight hundred English-speaking Chinese boys and a detachment of senior girls from Fairfield Girls' School, I experienced the same inspiration as when I spoke at Nelson Boys' College in New Zealand in 1931. The sight of those teenage schoolboys and girls filled me with a sense of call and I saw it as a great challenge and opportunity.

Other opportunities followed to speak to hundreds of senior-school pupils and university students and I also spoke at the True Light Church by interpretation. I found myself meeting English-speaking Chinese men of ability in positions of leadership who were mostly young and very open to the Gospel. I preached at Bethesda Katong Brethren Assembly where most of the leaders were under forty. Singapore had many schools and a large university whose graduates filled important positions in the educational world and in the thriving commercial life of this remarkable island state. On the Saturday evening I spoke to about forty church leaders and educationalists and then at a public meeting when some two hundred and fifty were present.

On arrival in Australia I told the story of Singapore and all its great potential for the future. A year later I urged Cecil Johnston, the leader of our work in India, to follow up the new openings. In the event it was no mere chance that he was held up for some time. He found open doors everywhere and a great response from over forty schools. He, in turn, stirred up the Australians, urging them to develop this new and important opportunity, to which they warmly responded. Today Singapore is a thriving Scripture Union centre with its own camp site and a gifted team of staff workers. It is also the focal point for the ANZEA (Australia, New Zealand and East Asia) region, covering Scripture Union activities in all countries from New Zealand in the south to Korea and Japan in the north.

The meeting of the all-Australia federal conference, with delegates from New Zealand, was held at the Scripture Union camp and conference centre in the Blue Mountains of New South Wales. This was, in some ways, the most important event of this 35,000 mile journey. It was significant because it met ten years after the memorable 1944 consultations described earlier, but it was now a strong, well-led movement in each Australian state.

The conference brought together some twenty leaders, chairmen, council members and senior staff from New Zealand and all the Australian states, under the able chairmanship of Alan Kerr. On the final Easter Sunday afternoon, the federal council of Australia was officially launched. This was a giant step forward and prepared the way for the great missionary outreach when Australia and New Zealand joined forces with the Chinese leadership in Singapore to form ANZEA.

Once again the principle was established that a well-organised and spiritually strong base can be stimulated to reach out and activate new developments over a vast area. But the base itself must not become selfish and self-centred and it must be strong enough to carry the weight of its new responsibilities. It seemed that the foundations, so slowly and painfully laid in 1944 had not been in vain.

Following Old Jordans, I was invited to visit South Africa in 1960/61. It was felt that the time was ripe for a forward move and I set off in late December with much anticipation.

On the way to Cape Town, brief visits were paid to Nairobi, Salisbury and Bulawayo. In each of these centres, Scripture Union and CSSM had been well established for many years and it was a joy to see something of their activities.

Arrangements had been made for me to see the Victoria

Falls and the Wankie Game Reserve, but an unexpected encounter with the memory of David Livingstone proved to be even more significant. It was early morning and still dark when I set off to find the Falls. This was easy, as the unceasing thunder of the mighty waterfall soon filled my ears. Walking through the trees in the dawn light, I came across a statue of David Livingstone at the point where the Zambesi poured foaming into the chasm below. He seemed to be striding through the trees, shoulders slightly hunched forward and then to have stopped, feet firmly planted in his big boots, as if he had seen the Falls for the first time. His strong rugged face under his famous cap looked out across the river, and his long legs seemed to be about to carry him forward as if on one of his famous journeys. His right hand held his walking stick and his left his Bible supported on his water bottle and partly open somewhere in the New Testament with his fingers tucked in as if to keep the place.

As I watched, the sun rose and its light shone through the huge plumes of spray. It is not surprising that the Africans called it 'the smoke that thunders'. I turned to read the words of the plaque behind me which recorded that:

'On the 100th Anniversary of the discovery of the Falls on 16th November, 1855, men and women of all races in and from all parts of the Federation of Rhodesia and Nyasaland, assembled solemnly to dedicate themselves and their country to carry on the high Christian aims and ideals which inspired David Livingstone in his mission here'.

I felt a joyful sense of God's presence in this place and, looking back over my life, I realise that this has been so on several occasions when confronted by the beauty and grandeur of nature.

Sitting at Livingstone's feet I turned to that morning's SU reading which was from Hebrews 12:1–2, and which I had brought with me to read during the course of the morning: 'Therefore, since we are surrounded by so great a cloud of witnesses . . . let us run with perseverance the race that is set before us, looking unto Jesus the pioneer and perfecter of our faith . . .'

I turned away reluctantly, carrying with me the memory of a great spiritual experience which was to prepare me for the important days that lay ahead in South Africa. Longfellow's words may be hackneyed but they fitted my mood:

> Lives of great men all remind us
> We can make our lives sublime,
> And, departing, leave behind us
> Footprints on the sands of time.

The official side of the visit to South Africa began with a conference with the staff members at Pretoria, under the leadership of Paul Reed, the general secretary. At that conference and in the seventeen days which followed, there were many useful discussions. Both Paul and his chairman, Otto Dose, had been at the Old Jordans' conference and had returned to South Africa imbued with its spirit and convinced of the value of its constitutional arrangements.

I soon found that the Scripture Union and CSSM family in South Africa consisted of men and women of high calibre, both as council members, staff members, friends and supporters. Many in leading positions were the fruits of Frank Millard's camps for boys and missions for children.

The full council met at the small seaside resort of Fish Hoek on December 26th. The meeting lasted from nine a.m. to five p.m., and in that time the council members adopted a series of decisions which put the whole movement throughout South Africa on a completely new footing. Local committees were given increased responsibility and long-term plans were agreed for regional developments, adequate staffing and financial support. Also a new emphasis was given to schools work on a much wider basis than before. These and other reforms and rearrangements were decided upon so easily and fittingly that I was astonished. This was partly due to careful preparation and also because the council members, mostly in their early forties, were accustomed to efficient committee work and firm decision-making, and were open to new ideas under good chairmanship. To my great joy they adopted in full and without emendation the decisions of the Old Jordans' conference. We seemed to accomplish as much in a single day as might have taken months or years in some other countries. This can happen when God's time comes and when, at that moment, God's people are ready to hear and obey.

Up to 1961, spasmodic attempts had been made to open up work among the coloured and black communities but these efforts had been unsuccessful. In the years that followed, new developments gradually opened up in this respect, so that at the time of writing, unrestricted opportunities are available for evangelism among all ethnic groups in South Africa, with black and white brothers in Christ serving together as members of the staff.

As an extension of our contacts with our friends from many countries our home became a minor training school for new staff members mainly from the European continent. They came to us from Switzerland, France, Germany, Holland, Belgium, Scandinavia and Portugal to learn or improve their English and to absorb all they could about the history, ideals and methods of our movement. It was a great experience to make so many new friends, to learn at first hand about different cultures and ways of doing things. Our children shared fully in these friendships and benefited greatly as a result. During the year of the Old Jordans' conference we were never without visitors from May through to October, assisted by a hospitality grant from the council. For me it was all quite reminiscent of my own childhood when our hospitable Kilmacolm home entertained a steady stream of weekend preachers and missionaries from many countries.

During the 1957 Easter holidays Marion, Janet (aged sixteen), Elizabeth (aged fourteen), and I visited a large exhibition in Brussels. One memory stands out vividly, the Israeli exhibition. Near to it was the Russian offering, a huge glass and steel building with severe and regular lines, imposing but cold and impersonal. It contained exhibits of heavy machinery and technology. Each country had its characteristic display. The Israeli one was among the smallest. We were met at the entrance by a young Jewish woman who led us up a gently sloping walkway where, on either side, the walls were entirely covered with frescoes depicting the sufferings, imprisonments and indignities meted out to the Jewish people in various periods of history. As we continued to walk up the slope we saw at the far end suspended from the ceiling a large glass object rather like a diamond. As we approached it we could see inside it a symbolic facsimile in gold representing the ideal of the New Jerusalem, the City of God.

Here once again, as so often in Jewish history, was the vision to which all their journeys and strivings were directed. For them the hope and vision was, and still is, the earthly Jerusalem, while for us as Christians our hopes are set on 'a city which has foundations whose builder and maker is God', and on the vision of the Kingdom of Christ in the hearts of men and women, individually and collectively.

My response was acute and personal. I was among those who were being drawn upwards by the dream of the Kingdom of Christ, the true Messiah, ruling, guiding, shepherding, leading, comforting and re-creating His children. In the experience of the new birth our eyes are open to *see* the Kingdom as expressed in the community of the people of God in the local church and in the specialist societies and task forces raised up to fulfil their distinctive roles.

15 EVANGELICAL ALLIANCE

Some years before the possibility of retirement appeared on the horizon I began to make a list of things to do. The list grew slowly over the years and when I came to tot it up I was astonished to find that it numbered about fifty items. Writing a book came near to the bottom of the list and was only a remote likelihood. It was only at the repeated suggestions of several friends that I undertook the task.

My reasons for retiring in 1968 were in part influenced by memories of T. B. Bishop and J. H. Hubbard, both of whom had held on for too long. It seemed best to pull out when everything was going well and to err on the side of retiring too soon rather than too late. Also, I wanted to retire at an age when it would be possible to take on some less exacting, but nevertheless worthwhile task. It was no mere chance that my next job was well calculated to keep me humble.

It is important that a man in a leading position and approaching retirement should not move out until arrangements have been made for his successor. In our case the search for the right man occupied several years and resulted in the appointment of Nigel Sylvester.

Nigel had been converted while a student at Cambridge through the ministry of the American preacher, Donald Gray Barnhouse. He was drawn into the fellowship of the mission at East Runton CSSM in Norfolk, which was his first introduction to Scripture Union. Following outstanding success at Cambridge in mathematics and then theological training at Ridley Hall, he joined the staff of the CSSM for service in West Africa. He concentrated mainly on Ghana where a programme of school visitations and camps during the holidays resulted in the formation of SU groups, and consequently a new generation of educated young Christians going up to the universities and entering the professions.

From these men of ability a council was formed consisting almost entirely and, later, wholly of Ghanian nationals.

Scripture Union membership has a long history in many parts of Africa, but these developments brought new life and a completely new approach. What was achieved in Ghana was typical of new growth in more than twenty African countries, in each of which the leadership had been wisely chosen and trained.

It was only after careful deliberation that the council was led to invite Nigel to succeed me. Like myself twenty-two years earlier he found himself in a dilemma, for he did not want to leave the work in Africa where he had been so happy. After much heart-searching, however, he accepted the council's invitation.

Before leaving Africa he met and married Mary Cawston who had been teaching French in Ghana. As Nigel's wife, Mary has backed him in his many responsibilities. After completing a year's training Nigel succeeded me under the new title of general director in England in April 1968. It was a very happy experience to hand over the reins of office to such a valued friend and capable leader. And so, with the general directorship settled, it was now time for me to make my own plans.

In May 1965 I was asked to join the council of the Evangelical Alliance. My first contact with EA had been a visit to Mr. Martyn Gooch, in 1948, who was then the elderly secretary. At that time the EA was in the doldrums but later, under the leadership first of Roy Cattell and then of Gilbert Kirby, it blossomed into new life and effectiveness. During the fifties a leading part was played by Jack Dain who later became a bishop in Sydney, Hugh Gough, later Archbishop of Sydney, Gilbert Kirby, and the chairman, Sir Arthur Smith. They were all men I very much admired. I also appreciated the EA because of its long history dating back to 1846, of its concern for the Kingdom of God as a whole, and for the way in which it saw itself playing its distinctive part in that wide concept. It is all too easy for us to be limited in our outlook to some sectional interest, our local church, a particular missionary society or some charity, but it is good to be encouraged to think in terms of the Kingdom of God as a whole, thus I saw in the EA the nearest approach to an evangelical ecumenical movement. I had received a number of requests to serve on councils and help in other ways, but none of these appealed so much as the EA and I therefore willingly accepted their invitation.

All I had to do at first was to attend the meetings of the council and make an occasional contribution to the discussion. The time came, however, when Gilbert Kirby, after ten years as general secretary, was appointed principal of the London Bible College. He was succeeded by my friend and former SU colleague, Morgan Derham.

These were turbulent times in the evangelical world. Things came to a head in October 1966, at a public meeting in the Central Hall, Westminster, held under EA auspices, when Dr. Martyn Lloyd Jones made an eloquent appeal for evangelical churches and individual evangelicals to come together, to stand together as churches, to work together, and to bear witness together. He recognised that this would involve some evangelicals leaving the Church of England and other comprehensively constituted churches, in the interests of evangelical unity; but he believed that if this were done it would be right to expect the Spirit of God to come upon us in mighty revival and blessing.

In 1967, Westminster Chapel, under Dr. Lloyd Jones's leadership, resigned from the Congregational Union, and joined the Fellowship of Independent Evangelical Churches. The separation issue continued to be debated and the situation was made more difficult by some journalistic-type treatment in the Christian press.

At the National Evangelical Anglican Congress (NEAC) in 1967, when the Rev. John Stott was chairman, the members of the conference, numbering about one thousand, decided against any form of secession from the Church of England and committed themselves to fight the battle for evangelicalism within the structures of the national Church. This important policy decision gave them a new objective and increased their cohesiveness, but it sharpened the lines of separation from their evangelical brethren in the non-anglican world.

In the years that followed Dr. Lloyd Jones's earnest and sincere appeal, the result was not greater evangelical unity, but increasing separation of most Independent Free Churches from those evangelicals who felt it right to remain within the

174

more comprehensive churches. This new sense of freedom to go ahead on their own, together with the leadership of John Stott, helps to account for the remarkable flowering of the evangelical Anglican movement in its present form. Similarly evangelicals in the Methodist, Baptist and United Reformed Churches have organised their own groupings within their denominations.

In all these debates and discussions there was very little in the way of personal recrimination or bitter personal attacks on individuals. There may have been a few instances of this at local level and in some respects in the Christian press but it was not so between the main leaders.

This is an old problem, at least as old as the history of the Christian Church, whether to try to reform from within where reform is needed, or to 'come out and be separate' in the interests of doctrinal purity and perhaps to endure the obloquy of being 'without the camp'. Those who advocate reform from within run the risk of compromising their identity and their message, while those who insist on separation and independence sometimes tend to become isolated splinter groups characterised by a lifeless legalism. Advocates of opposing opinions claim scriptural authority and are prepared to argue their case, but in real-life situations the issues are usually complex.

Many of us remain for life within whatever church structure we were born into, only changing under compelling circumstances. Temperament also enters into these decisions. Some feel the need for spontaneous informality, others dignity, beauty and order. Some favour music and art forms, others meditative silence, intellectual satisfaction or authoritative teaching. The influence and teaching of someone gifted with strong powers of leadership and persuasion is also significant.

In 1968, the EA was faced with internal difficulties. We lost Morgan Derham's leadership, and the search for his successor was far from easy. Someone remarked at the time, 'Who wants that bed of nails!' To make matters worse, we found ourselves in severe financial difficulties concerning the offices at 30 Bedford Place.

I was chairman of the council at the time and along with others we found ourselves involved in a rescue operation.

It came as an answer to prayer when we heard that the Hebrew Christian Alliance was selling its freehold property at 19 Draycott Place, near Sloane Square. In a remarkably short time we were able to purchase this freehold property for £31,000 with the help of a large mortgage. Under this arrangement the outgoings amounted to approximately £2,200 per annum as compared with a rental of £2,800 if we had remained at Bedford Place. This building was newer and in some respects better than the previous one, and gave us the security of a freehold property which was also increasing in value.

In 1969 a new general secretary had been found in the person of Gordon Landreth. His first year was difficult, but Gordon's cool and steady wisdom prevailed. It could be said of him, 'I am among you as one that serveth.' His humble, quiet diplomacy and hard work gradually gained him a respected place in the evangelical world at home and abroad. Educated at Oxford, he had served as an administration officer in the government of Malawi (then Nyasaland) and subsequently as secretary of the graduates' fellowship of the Universities and Colleges Christian Fellowship.

During my two years as president of the EA I represented the Alliance at various meetings and conferences. Over the years, the Evangelical Alliance has promoted many important activities, including the Annual Week of Prayer, the National Assemblies of Evangelicals, the promotion of evangelism, ministers' conferences, provision of channels of communication at home and abroad within the evangelical world.

The Evangelical Alliance has also served as midwife to a number of important organisations which, after some initial help, have become independent organisations in their own right. Among these could be included Hostels for Overseas Students, Tear Fund (the Evangelical Alliance Relief Fund), the Arts Centre Group and the Evangelical Missionary Alliance. The EA also helped to launch the first Billy Graham Crusades. They formed the EA radio committee and their efforts to build bridges between the more independent types of churches should not be forgotten.

Towards the end of July 1969 I awoke one night with the uncomfortable sensation that my heart was being held in a tight grip. This was combined with rather a violent irregular cardiac action. I recognised the symptoms of acute auricular fibrillation, later confirmed by a heart specialist.

I felt as if I was about to lose consciousness, and then as if I was about to die. I was surprised to find that this did not worry me. When not preoccupied with the alarming physical symptoms, I thought about death, and was quite surprised at my reaction. I found myself thinking, 'This is interesting — I've sometimes wondered what it would be like to die, and what would lie beyond. Now I'm about to find out.' I was a little disappointed at this reaction which was that of satisfying an almost scientific inquisitiveness rather than a spiritual experience or the beautific vision. It was so unlike my mother's triumphant death when heaven seemed to be opened before her. I came to realise increasingly that the death of the body is not the end of the story but the beginning of a new chapter, the details of which remain closed to us until God turns the page.

I made a quick recovery and was glad to have been given a further lease of life, but slightly disappointed that I had not been granted at least a glimpse of what lies beyond.

16   THE SPIRITUAL GLOW

James Moffat's translation of Romans 12:11, 'Maintain the spiritual glow', provides the theme for this chapter and helps to define our spiritual aspirations.

During the difficulties of the early years in London I often set aside Thursday mornings as times of prayer and thought about whatever aspects of our work most needed unhurried attention. This proved to be of great value. Sometimes the morning ended with a clue to the solution of some difficult problem, or with a sense of guidance as to the next step to be taken, or perhaps with a fresh inspiration and accession of courage to continue. There were also times of barrenness and disappointment, but for the most part I proved the truth of the words of R. C. Trench, Archbishop of Dublin (1807–1886):

Lord what a change within us
One short hour spent in Thy presence can prevail to make,
What heavy burdens from our bosoms take;
What parchèd ground refresh as with a shower.
We kneel how weak, we rise how full of power.
Why therefore should we do ourselves this wrong
Or others, that we are not always strong,
That we are overborne with care,
Anxious or troubled, when with us is prayer,
And joy and strength and courage are with Thee.

It was never easy in a busy life to set aside and use these times. One often had to fight the battle of the threshold, for it might take up to an hour to overcome wandering thoughts and to bring the mind and spirit into the atmosphere of the sanctuary. In later years when the pressures and problems were less, I gradually dropped the practice, reverting to a much shorter daily 'quiet time'.

While it is necessary to maintain a high level of individual spiritual life and fervour, it is also important to do so in communities and corporate bodies. In Scripture Union we tried to do this in various ways. The Tuesday meeting of heads of departments had much to do with it, when we met together, discussed, argued, and above all prayed. Then every two years we had a staff conference. All field staff were expected to attend and as many as could be spared from the office. We lived together for three full days, eating together, playing, talking, praying, hearing the Word of God, and finally sharing together at the Lord's table. Some individual departments had weekends away from time to time, and prayer and fellowship conferences were arranged in the regions for both staff and supporters. We owe a great debt to the large number of friends, most of whom we never meet, but who support us faithfully by their prayers. And perhaps most important of all, those of us who were senior tried to give a lead to our younger colleagues and the new arrivals.

The Scripture Union's internationally recognised emblem of the lamp and the flame can be a constant reminder of the need to maintain the warm glow and the steady light lest the spiritual life in any fellowship of God's people should flicker and die. The firm structure of the lamp exists to service and replenish the flame, but the interior reservoir needs constant refilling.

Much has already been said about the importance of correct structure, but structure is a useless thing unless it is suffused with life and energy, and it is a dead thing unless it is given a 'human face'. In his letter to the Ephesians (2:21, 22) Paul refers to the need for both structure and spirit: 'The household of God, built upon the foundation of the apostles and prophets, Christ Jesus Himself being the corner stone, in whom the *structure* is joined together and grows into a holy temple in the Lord; in whom you also are built into it for a dwelling place of God in the *Spirit*.'

We may try to define this quality of life in the community as an inward transformation and constant renewal of spiritual life resulting in a warm, loving, caring community expressing itself individually and corporately in genuine goodness, practical service and effective witness. As morale is to an army keenness in business, team spirit in sport, so but on a higher plane, is the fervent glow of spiritual life to the fellowship of the people of God, whether in a local church or in a specialised arm of the church such for instance as the missionary societies and the youth movements.

The first essential in maintaining a high level of spirituality in any community is the quality of the life of its leadership. Spiritual life of the group or fellowship is not likely to rise higher than the level of the spiritual life of its leaders.

Many hardworking Christian leaders have become weighed down by burdens of administration and finance and have lost the spiritual freshness and warmth that characterised their earlier days, and this spiritual decline in the leadership will inevitably spread to the fellowship as a whole. The spiritual leader must be a pastor to his colleagues, a task in which he will carry heavy burdens but also reap rich rewards of love and fellowship. If he is wise he will freely share the burden of pastoral and teaching responsibility with others, and encourage some who have these gifts to exercise them increasingly. He may not be able to escape entirely from administrative responsibilities but these should be delegated as far as possible and it is essential that he should not be burdened with a mass of detail.

There are two classic examples of this in scripture. In Exodus chapter 18, Moses is described as being overwhelmed in dealing with minor disputes, and when Jethro, his father-in-law, saw what was happening he warned Moses that he would wear himself out, and counselled him:

You shall represent the people before God, and bring their cases to God; and you shall teach them the statutes and the decisions and make them to know the way they must walk and what they must do. Moreover choose able men from all the people, such as fear God, men who are trustworthy and who hate a bribe; and place such men over the people as rulers of thousands, of hundreds, of fifties, and of tens and let them judge the people at all times; every great matter they shall bring to you, but any small matter they shall decide themselves; so it will be easier for you, and they will bear the burden with you. If you do this, and God so command you, then you will be able to endure and all this people will go to their place in peace.

The New Testament example of the same principle occurs in Acts when a dispute arose about widows who were being overlooked in the daily distribution.

> So the Twelve called the whole body of disciples together and said, 'It would be a grave mistake for us to neglect the Word of God in order to wait at table. Therefore, friends, look out seven men of good reputation from your number, men full of the Spirit and of wisdom, and we will appoint them to deal with these matters, while we devote ourselves to prayer and the ministry of the Word.' This proposal proved acceptable to the whole body. (Acts 6:2–4, N.E.B.)

Thus the teaching, evangelistic and spiritual ministries of the church were preserved and enhanced.

In the Old Testament the leadership of God's people was in fact in the form of a triumvirate of prophets, priests and kings. Ideally the priests were the men of God who led the people in worship, headed by the High Priest who bore the names of the twelve tribes on his breast. Their duty was to maintain the warm glow of spiritual worship, first in the Tabernacle in the wilderness and later in the Temple at Jerusalem. Then there were the prophets who proclaimed the Word of God in the contemporary situations calling the people to repentance, righteousness and spiritual renewal. The function of the king was that of administration; he was the focal point of order and justice and was responsible for the overall leadership.

Sadly in each case there were many examples of serious failure. Only too often the priests failed in their duty and became formal and spiritually dead. There were true prophets who were men of God, but there were also false prophets, and saddest of all were many kings who did evil in the sight of the Lord. Yet in spite of much failure these three-fold offices were retained, until at last, with the coming of the true Messiah, all three for the first and last time were fulfilled in one person.

But on the human level it would be unreasonable to expect these three qualities to be combined in one personality. So when one of the elements is lacking, prayerful search should be made until the gap can be filled. Both Scripture and practical experience point to the desirability of having a well-balanced team under the guidance of a wise and experienced leader carefully chosen by his colleagues and loyally supported by them.

There are many warnings in Scripture against the dangers of corporate back-sliding and loss of spiritual life and power. In the prophecy of Ezekiel, chapters ten and eleven, there is a vivid description of the glory of the Lord in the form of a dazzling light departing from the Temple as if reluctantly, first from the threshold, then from the east gate, then from the midst of the city, then to stand upon the mountain to the east side of the city, and thus the Temple was left like a body without a soul. But later the glory was restored, and Ezekiel saw that 'the glory of the Lord came from the east; and the sound of His coming was like the sound of many waters; and the earth shone with His glory . . . and behold the glory of the Lord filled the Temple.' It is easily possible for an individual or a movement to drift spiritually without realising what is happening. An imperceptible lowering of standards and an unconscious spiritual decline can set in, together with a cooling in spiritual devotion. It was said of Samson that, 'The Lord had departed from him *and he knew it not*,' and Hosea described Ephraim's decline as 'his head is sprinkled with grey *but he does not notice.*'

Perhaps the most vivid example in the New Testament comes from the book of Revelation, chapter two, in a letter to the church at Ephesus, 'But I have this against you that you have abandoned the love you had at first.'

It was Dr. Oswald Smith of Toronto who remarked that the history of many a religious organisation could be summed up as beginning with a man of God with a burning heart. Then a movement develops, which is taken over by the machinery of a sterile organisation, and this finally slows down and comes to a halt ending as a lifeless museum. What began as a flame ends as a trail of smoke, the torrent becomes a trickle and the mountain stream ends in mud.

The following is an interesting example from the history of the church. Olive Wyon in her book *Living Springs* (SCM Press) tells the story. In the year 1112 St. Bernard arrived at the Monastery of Citeaux in France. By his brilliant leadership he soon put Citeaux on the map. As a Cistercian his aim was simply to seek God in contemplation and to live the whole of his life to His glory.

For a time the new Order flourished exceedingly, both inwardly and outwardly. But by 1250 there were signs of decline. The Black Death and the Hundred Years War affected it profoundly. But these events were not the cause of its decline: that was at work secretly for a long time. This was due in part to the very virtues of the Cistercian Order; the monks had gone into trade with such success that their monasteries had become wealthy. They had to market great supplies of wheat and wine, oil and wool. They had to do business on a large scale with large warehouses and commercial agencies. Monks had to make long journeys for business purposes; some, for instance, had to travel on river boats to ship cargoes of wine from the Moselle down the Rhine to Holland. The result was that though these men continued to lead exemplary lives and used their riches to help the poor and sick, they became so busy and active that the spirit of prayer evaporated. The body was still there "doing good" but the spirit had gone out of it.'

Mr. G. W. Gibb, former general director of the China Inland Mission, told me that when he was a young man in Aberdeen the Y.M.C.A. was a flourishing and spiritually effective organisation. When the city of Aberdeen appointed a Lord Provost who was a committed Christian he was invited to join the board of the Y.M.C.A. and did so helpfully. When a new Lord Provost took office, a man with no particular Christian convictions, he replaced his predecessor on the board, and it became the regular practice to include successive Lord Provosts. 'From that day,' said my wise old counsellor, 'from that day the spiritual power and influence of the Aberdeen Y.M.C.A. declined. So,' he added, looking me straight in the eye, 'never put anyone on your board or governing body who is not fully in support of your spiritual objectives and standards.' Then, with great emphasis, 'Don't do it.'

Cardinal Basil Hume in *Searching for God* (Hodder and Stoughton) comments on the tension between the marketplace and the desert:

'By the desert I mean the withdrawal from activity and people to meet God. By the market-place I mean involvement in pastoral situations of one kind or another . . . Should we be in the desert, withdrawn, or should we be in the market-place involved? St. Augustine talking about bishops says that while love of truth drives a man to seek holy leisure, the demands of charity demand his involvement: Now the market-place is distracting. Of itself it has attractions and in it we find responsibilities to be carried out. We can too, escape to the market-place because we fear the desert, because we are fearful of solitude, fearful of silence; because we are fearful to face the demands and claims which God might make, indeed does make, upon us. We shall never be safe in the market-place unless we are at home in the desert.'

It is not uncommon to find that in many local churches and Christian organisations there are some who are called to a special ministry of intercession. Perhaps for one reason or another they are shut in from the busy world and find fulfilment in such a ministry. The influence of these praying people is invaluable. To know that we are being prayed for, and to pray for others in turn, is a blessing indeed. In this way invisible networks of love and fellowship are created, and a quality of spiritual warmth suffuses the whole community. But such a ministry of intercession is not easy and can be costly, and indeed the same is true of all forms of spiritual leadership.

> There is no gain but by a loss.
> You cannot save but by a cross —
> The corn of wheat to multiply
> Must fall into the ground and die.
> Wherever you ripe fields behold,
> Waving to God their sheaves of gold,
> Be sure some corn of wheat has died —
> Some soul has there been crucified;
> Someone has wrestled, wept and prayed,
> And fought hell's legions undismayed.

A high spiritual tone and the prevention of decline in any community of believers can only be maintained by the diligent use of the means of grace. This will include the whole community worshipping thoughtfully, seriously and joyfully, celebrating together and 'Keeping the feast', hearing the Word of God, praying and singing together and also carrying out these activities in smaller and more intimate groups. And in all things and by all means, encouraging, caring, sharing, forgiving, serving and relaxing together; and then when scattered abroad in the world to love our neighbour and in some small measure to be living 'Christs' to our fellowmen.

17 NO MERE CHANCE

In the present age the immensely powerful idea that all religion, and indeed all life, is meaningless threatens Christians from all sides. Western civilisation was once based on the universally accepted idea of a natural and moral law under God, but the current humanist philosophy portrays man as an independent being with no external controls. The universe and the world of nature of which we are a part is considered to be one vast impersonal system moving forward relentlessly and inexorably towards some meaningless fate.

But now a fundamental change is taking place and it is coming not from the theologians but from the physicists and the philosophers. The tide began to turn with Einstein's Theory of Relativity in which he discarded the idea of a closed mechanistic universe. He describes his feelings as 'rapturous amazement at the harmony of natural law which reveals an intelligence of such superiority that, compared with it, all the systematic thinking and acting by human beings is an utterly insignificant reflection'. He added, 'I, at any rate, am convinced that He is not playing at dice.'

The story unfolded in this book reveals that, at least for the two main personalities described, the Christian life has not been meaningless. My wife and I look back on forty-eight years of marriage and family life, and more than forty-eight years of Christian service, with the strong conviction that for us life has not been the result of mere chance. We realise that for many of our contemporaries religion and life are meaningless. For them men and women are the victims of irresistible evolutionary forces as many thoughtful atheists and agnostics claim. That is the mood of the age in which we live, but it is not the mood of the Christian, for we believe that men and women, and indeed children, are free to make life choices which are full of meaning and purpose. For us the life of faith is a life of fulfilment, not fatalism, and despite doubts and puzzlements, and indeed partly because of them, we can grow in understanding and spiritual maturity.

During the decade of the sixties while some theologians were proclaiming that 'God is dead' (that very idea is now out of theological fashion) the physicists and cosmologists and more recently some philosophers were moving in the opposite direction. Professor T. F. Torrance, for twenty-seven years Professor of Christian Dogmatics at New College, Edinburgh, after describing the Newtonian view of the universe as a closed system, mechanistic in character, now reports that, since Einstein,

'the old post-Darwin conflict between science and religion is a thing of the past; that science, rather than being the sworn enemy of a religious outlook, is now its ally; that the sciences of physics and cosmology especially, support the Christian understanding; that science now makes for profession of faith rather than its rejection. It is the scientists, especially the physicists and mathematicians in the universities, who are now becoming believers.'

He adds that new discoveries about the origins of the universe are forcing scientists to ask theologians basic questions about the universe of which we are a part. A layman's impression of the contrast between the Biblical view and that of many scientists could be expressed as follows:

	Modern Science	The Biblical Revelation
When did the universe begin?	Don't know	'In the beginning God . . .' (Genesis 1:1.)
How did it begin?	Don't know	'God created the heavens and the earth' (Genesis 1:1.)
Why was it started?	Don't know	'God created man in his own image' and gave him dominion. (Genesis 1:27, 28.)
Where did all this vast energy come from?	Don't know	'The raging ocean that covered everything was engulfed in total darkness and the power of God was moving over the water. Then God commanded, "let there be light".' (Genesis 1:2.)
How will it end?	Don't know	We wait for new heavens and a new earth in which righteousness dwells. (2 Peter 3:13.)
CONCLUSION: Did it all evolve by mere chance?	Yes.	No!

If it were not presumptuous, we Christians might have been excused for saying 'we told you so', for we have never believed that we are the products of blind fate. For us life is not meaningless, but in fact is packed with meaning. We believe that the hairs of our head are numbered and that we are of more value than many sparrows. We believe that when we dedicate our lives to the will of God we can see His guiding and restraining hand in all the affairs of our lives. The signs of the zodiac have no hold upon us, nor has the number thirteen; we have no need to touch wood, cross our fingers or find our horoscope in the daily papers.

Some people seem to feel that it is wrong and unspiritual to have doubts of any kind. The answer to this depends upon the kind of doubt of which we are thinking. There is, on the one hand, such a thing as pathological doubt which, like pathological guilt, can be classified as mental and emotional illness associated with depression, suffering and insecurity. Then there are the doubts which arise from spiritual malnutrition and a neglect of worship, prayer, Bible study, reading and Christian fellowship. This can result in one's spiritual sensitivities becoming blunted, faith is weakened and doubt takes hold. Thirdly, there are the healthy doubts of a questioning mind which asks some of the most basic questions and wrestles with the problems in a spirit of faith and hope, of finding an answer which will open up new vistas of truth, and the discovery of rich stores of spiritual and mental wealth, and a stronger and more stimulating faith. Many great men and women of faith have reached the heights only by going through the depths.

For the Christian the Bible unfolds a philosophy of life in which we can see the interweaving of God's self-revelation and man's search for meaning in history, nature and human experience. However much we may differ in details of interpretation, the broad Biblical theme in favour of meaning and purpose is overwhelming, from the opening sentence of Genesis 'In the beginning God . . .' to the last chapter of Revelation where the Lord Jesus is spoken of as, 'The Alpha and the Omega, the first and the last, the beginning and the end.' There is, however, a startling exception in the book of Ecclesiastes which gives us a cautionary insight into what it must feel like to be a hardened sceptic full of pessimism, despair and cynicism, and because his outlook is bounded by the horizons of the material world he has to conclude that, 'all is emptiness and vexation of spirit'.

Running throughout the whole of Scripture are the two great doctrines of divine sovereignty and human responsibility. There are times in our lives when we are conscious of the over-ruling sovereignty of God when He takes the initiative in our affairs. For instance, had I not fallen ill with scarlet fever in the winter of 1930 and been sent to an isolation hospital for six weeks with plenty of time to reflect, I might well have lost the sense of the call of God and might have missed the great opportunities for service which lay ahead.

When our little Alistair was born into our family we accepted this as part of the over-ruling providence of God, but we also had to play our part in accepting responsibility for caring for him. Although shockingly deformed physically his little life was no mere accident. His sweet and cheerful nature shone through his physical handicap like glimpses of sunshine, and he brought a quality of love and tenderness into our family which was unique and which we could never have experienced otherwise. No one could ever persuade us that his little life was meaningless.

I look across at my wife quietly knitting in her old arm-chair (bought for twenty-two shillings and sixpence nearly fifty years ago in a second-hand furniture shop in Wellington) and thinking about one or other of her eleven grandchildren. I say to myself *she* is not the result of mere chance, nor is she part of a closed mechanistic system with no power of choice, no responsibility for her decisions, the automatic product of chance and environment. So long as there are people like her in the world I refuse to believe that everything in our lives has been the result of blind chance. She knits quietly on without saying a word, but there comes from her busy creative hands a steady flow of knitted garments for her friends and grand-children. Her busy needles are knitting up love and meaning and purpose to a carefully planned design; the colours have been carefully chosen to blend with the pattern. Thus our two lives have been knit into the pattern of life as described in this book. I firmly believe that it has been no mere chance.

189

I have sometimes heard friends in moments of happiness remark, 'The Lord has been good to me.' I think I know what they mean, and it is certainly good to be thankful for all God's mercies, but what of those for whom life has been one long struggle with poverty, pain, depression ('worse than a thousand toothaches'), blighted love or other forms of human misery. As one young Christian, deeply distressed, cried through his tears, 'I have tried so hard to be good (and he had, I knew that) and why should this happen to me?' I tried to retrace for him the old story of Job and to comfort him with some of the exceeding great and precious promises of Scripture, and above all tried to be a good listener. As the months went by healing slowly came.

It does seem as if life is not fair, and it is no use pretending that it is, but this is not to say that we are the victims of blind chance, and that we are powerless to do anything about it. Many examples can be quoted of men and women afflicted with some of the severest handicaps in life who, by the grace of God and immense effort and courage, have not only triumphed over the disabilities, but transmuted them into lives of great rarity and beauty.

Those who stood by the cross of Jesus could see no meaning or purpose in what was happening. Even for the friends of Jesus it was a meaningless tragedy; for the Roman soldiers a bloody incident in an ordinary day's work. But for Christians it has been the greatest event in human history.

> Through victory like defeat
> He won the meed and crown,
> Trod all His foes beneath His feet
> By being trodden down.

I still treasure in my commonplace book, which I started as long ago as 1923, the following extract from an old letter:

The main end of life is not to *do* but to *become*. For this we are being moulded and disciplined every hour. You cannot understand why year after year the stern ordeal is perpetuated; you think the time is wasted, you are doing nothing. Yes, but you are situated in the set of circumstances

190

that gives you the best opportunity for manifesting and therefore acquiring the qualities in which your character is naturally deficient. And the Refiner sits patiently beside the crucible intent upon the process, tempering the heat and eager that the scum should pass off and that His face should become perfectly reflected in the surface.

By contrast perhaps the most dangerous times for the Christian are when everything seems to be going well. In times of slackness and ease there are no challenges to face and no big decisions to take. The rot can easily set in and character and personality degenerate.

Ideally the Christian is one who lives a life of commitment, above all to the Lordship of Christ and the Biblical view of life. This whole-hearted willingness to long-term commitment extends to marriage and family life, to the Church and the Kingdom of God, to friendship and service for others and to witness in the world.

The Christian does not stand aside, aloof and uncaring, but involves himself in the spirit of his Master in the joys and sorrows of his fellow men and women. As for me this commitment to Christ began while I was still a child at the age of seven, was deepened as a schoolboy at the Lochearnhead camp, in marriage and Christian service, and in many of the crises and turning points of life.

There are many basic questions that occur to us as we reflect on life's experiences. I find myself at times trying to rethink some of the great central doctrines of the Christian faith; the nature of God, the trinity, the incarnation, the cross and the resurrection, the second coming of Christ, the Holy Spirit, ultimate human destiny and the problem of pain. In meditating on these and other great themes one is often out of one's depth, while at other times new insights and discoveries shine with sparkling brilliance, bringing deep satisfaction, hope and comfort. In our Sunday morning meetings for worship and in times of private meditation and prayer, these and other great truths are whole-heartedly believed in and gladly received by faith. In these moments of worship mental struggles can be put to one side and we can rejoice in what is positive and deeply satisfying. Faith and reason must go hand in hand, but there are moments when faith leaps ahead and reason struggles along behind.

It is right that we should give ourselves to thinking about questions of faith and doctrine and Christian commitment, but we cannot be preoccupied continually with them, for it is impossible to escape from the affairs of daily life and all the choices and decisions that have to be made in the market-place and at the office desk. In the greater issues of life it may seem superficially easy to solve these questions by shelving them, but if we do so we run the risk of having no further spiritual growth, no guiding star, no meaning or purpose. Much of the feeling of aimlessness in modern life comes about because so many people have no ultimate aim and seem unable to decide what life is for and what should be the final objective. This helps to account for the widespread incidence of depression in our modern society. To decide on an aim, to choose it deliberately and with care and to pursue it with diligence makes us men and women of character and purpose, provided we first choose our aim wisely; otherwise at the end of our days we shall look back and see that all our efforts have been in vain because the aim was false or unworthy. The challenge given by Joshua in his farewell to his people still holds good: 'Choose this day whom you will serve . . . but as for me and my house we will serve the Lord.' Not to choose is to choose, for choices are inescapable.

> 'It's the set of the sail and not the gale
> That determines the way we go.'

Pierre Loti speaks of those who still bow before the feet of Christ as those who go their way confident and calm. Writing somewhat wistfully as a non-Christian he continues, 'In default of this faith could we but anchor ourselves to some immortality . . . But there is nothing. Outside the ever shining personality of Christ everything is terror and darkness.'

But those of us who have put our faith in the living Christ have discovered the one sure anchorage, and despair is replaced by the greatest hope in the world.